MARLON BRANDO

Biography

MARLON
BRANDO

David Thomson

LONDON, NEW YORK, MUNICH,
MELBOURNE, and DELHI

DK PUBLISHING
Publisher Chuck Lang
Creative Director Tina Vaughan
Editorial Director Chuck Wills
Art Director Dirk Kaufman
Production Manager Chris Avgherinos
DTP Designer Milos Orlovic

First American Edition, 2003
2 4 6 8 10 9 7 5 3 1
Published in the United States
by DK Publishing, Inc.
375 Hudson Street
New York, New York 10014

produced by AVALON PUBLISHING GROUP, INC.
Project Editor Max Alexander
Senior Director, Editorial Will Balliett
Senior Director, Operations f-stop Fitzgerald
Photo Editor Tracy Armstead
Designer Lisa Vaughn
Assistant Editor Kristen Couse
Production Manager Mike Walters
Production Editor Simon Sullivan

A&E TELEVISION NETWORK
Director of Licensing Carrie Trimmer
Director Legal & Business Affairs Chey Blake
VP/GM Consumer Products & Merchandising Steve Ronson

A&E and Biography are trademarks of A&E Television Networks.
All Rights Reserved © 2003 AETN

Jacket design copyright © 2003 A&E Television Networks
and DK Publishing, Inc.
Text copyright © 2003 David Thomson

Photo Credits—See page 154

DK Publishing, Inc. offers special discounts for bulk purchases for
sales promotions or premiums. Specific, large-quantity needs can
be met with special editions, including personalized covers,
excerpts of existing guides, and corporate imprints. For more
information, contact Special Markets Department, DK Publishing,
Inc., 375 Hudson Street, New York, NY 10014 Fax: 212-689-5254.

Cataloging-in-Publication data is available from
the Library of Congress

ISBN 0-7894-9317-9

Reproduced by ColourScan, Singapore.
Printed and bound by R.R. Donnelley in the United States.

See our complete product line at
www.dk.com

Contents

Mirror for a Soul

B y 1971, Marlon Brando has already been written off in some quarters. He has done years of poor work, with an increasing reputation for willful irresponsibility. The studio making The Godfather, Paramount, has been so dismayed by young Francis Ford Coppola's insistence that this burned-out actor play the lead part that they have begun to lose faith in the director. So it is a production founded less in respect than in paranoia and suspicion. People expect Brando to be difficult.

But here in the opening, he has nothing to do at first but sit still in his chair, with a gray kitten on his lap—watching the intense, anxious face of a small-part player and wait while the camera draws back so slowly to reveal the sleek gun-metal of his hair, the full arc of his cheek and jowl, and the magisterial flutter of his right hand, not even in focus yet.

The fingers on that hand are stroking his cheek: you could surmise that the actor is still concerned about the arrangement of the rubber form in his mouth; or is the man, Vito Corleone, a little dandyish, a self-study, a performer, unable to stop drawing attention to himself? The small-part player tells a woeful story about a fine daughter, and boys who made her drink, and sought to take advantage of her. When she resisted, they beat her. This mortified father chokes back wrath and self-pity, and that's when Don Vito's languid hand makes the small gesture that brings the man a drink. It is the hand that, shortly, will be kissed by the visitor's desperate lips. This is the wedding day of Don Vito's daughter, and like a Sicilian—no matter that this is all in New York state—he can hardly refuse a friend's request. This father has not been a friend. Vito's sad, lazy voice remembers not one invitation to a cup of coffee, no matter that Don Vito's wife is the girl's godmother. The father didn't want to get into trouble. Don Vito accepts this. He is enormous and capacious in his understanding; it accounts for the enlargement in his cheeks, the fatalism that beholds all supplicants, and knows their scripted plea in advance. He touches his face, his hair, his cat, his chair; he is always making these small contacts. It is his way of establishing he is "there" and "here"; that he is power itself. But the actor must know that he is only a part of a mighty construct. He had to wait until the camera drew back enough to include him.

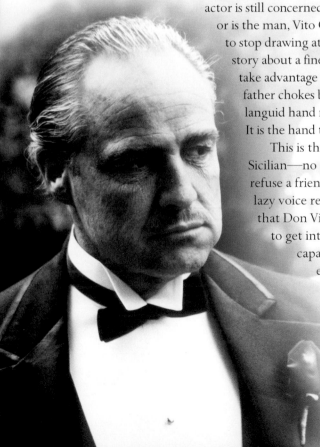

Better Late . . .
"From Brando I learned to come late," said *Godfather* co-star Al Pacino. He probably meant late to the set, but he might as well have been referring to Brando's spectacular comeback in the 1970s.

He must hear that the script has ironies (on the meaning of respect, say) that underline these grave scenes. He should know, if he is a diligent actor, that as Don Vito forgives and embraces this wounded, wronged father, and says, yes, justice will be done for his daughter's sake, but that may one day entail some small return, he must know that this man is an undertaker. And the actor knows what the character cannot quite know: that the service will prove to be a decent, artistic cosmetic job on the shattered corpse of Vito's own son, Sonny, the handsome brute who is looking on insolently from the gloom of this "Sicilian" parlor.

The structure of ironies is built in—that's how good The Godfather is. But this kind of foreboding, its sinister grace, is exactly in unison with the superb, calculated playing of the Don—such a human being, such a character, such an American, but a dandy, too, a man lost in self-love (how else can power and respect be so musical?), a man with a mirror for a soul. I mean an actor, for it is the skill of great actors to show us how everyone acts—ourselves included. Which is one reason these days why so many of us since 1971 have had such odd respect for the Mafia, for their discreet charm. The ones who only murder in style. It's like a Frenchman pretending to be Italian, and it's the opening to one of the great and most influential performances in American film: Marlon Brando as Vito Corleone.

Genius at Work

Brando (above, with Robert Duvall in the background) invented many of Don Corleone's mannerisms as the camera rolled. "I had never watched a genius at work before," said The Godfather's veteran producer, Al Ruddy.

Youth
1924–1941

GOD AND THE FATHER

There is no American film so filled with love and respect for fatherhood as *The Godfather*. Nor is this just the affection between a father and his own children—rather it is a paternalism and a shared purpose that extend to the wider reaches of family, to Italians battling in America and, from the very first words of the film, to being American, even if that code is not exactly the one in the Bill of Rights or written on the Statue of Liberty.

But if Vito Corleone is one of Marlon Brando's greatest moments, and one in which his shy hopes shine through on the surface of that dreaming face, then it has to be said that Brando and his real dad were forever in a kind of war. Yet evidently, the conflict was something Brando needed—if only to foster those deep hopes of what being a father might mean.

Marlon Brando Sr. had changed his named from Brandeaux or even possibly Brandow; it's not clear. The family line had come from out of Alsace, and the father had served in the American army in World War I. Though he settled his family (his wife, Marlon Jr., and two older daughters) at 3135 Mason Street in Omaha, Nebraska, the father was a traveling salesman. He was private, very fierce and intimidating, a blunt, rough man, a redneck some said. Exactly not the kind of father a sensitive boy needed— unless, sometimes, sensitivity needs to fight against the grain. The father daunted the boy, and he was inclined to pour anger on the household. That may be because he was criticized by his wife, Dorothy (or Dodie): for the father drank and paid for hookers in his hotel life on the road. You can say that he lived fancy-free, or you can see him as a sad drifter. But by the time Marlon was six, the father had a job as manager with the Calcium Carbonate Company, steady enough to move the family to Evanston, Illinois.

JOCELYN BRANDO

This lovely snapshot from New York in 1948 gives an uncanny sense of the affinity between brother and sister—Jocelyn and Marlon Brando (why were they never cast together in a great work?).

Born in 1919, Jocelyn Brando was the family member closest to Marlon. As they grew up, she was a protective older sister, who actually went to New York with him. She was also, for a moment at least, a promising actress herself. Indeed, she attracted a great deal of attention as the wife to Glenn Ford's cop in Fritz Lang's *The Big Heat* (1953)—it is that wife's shocking death, blown up in her own car, that prompts Ford's vengeful mission against the criminal syndicate. But Jocelyn's career never quite came together. She did a good deal of work on television (including a recurring role on *Dallas*), and she was also striking in two Brando pictures—*The Ugly American* and *The Chase*. She has not worked in the last twenty years.

Not that family life was ever serene. When Marlon was twelve, his father came home one night with lipstick on his clothes. There was a quarrel with his mother and his father attacked her physically. Marlon intervened and threatened to kill his own father.

Those things happen; in thought or dream, they make up the daily turmoil of adolescence. Beware of the kid who has not thought of destroying Dad. We can hardly know this father: he does not offer his own testimony for history—he did not know soon enough that he was to be the father of a great man; or perhaps he did not know how to establish himself against his son's bright light. So we see their dealings the way the son saw them—a tough, angry, boozy father who largely ignored the son: "He was a frightening, silent, brooding, angry, hard-drinking, rude man, a bully who loved to give orders and issue ultimatums—and he was just as tough as he talked. Perhaps that's why I've had a lifelong aversion to authority."

There are a lot of Marlon Brando stories to fit that claim: the kid in *The Wild One* who will rebel against whatever society offers; the outlaw in *One-Eyed Jacks* who is betrayed by his friend Dad Longworth, and who will eventually hunt that rascal down (and seduce his daughter); most famously of all there are the improvised passages in *Last Tango in Paris* in which Brando's character recalls the menacing and humiliating figure of his father, the man who made him work in animal manure, the man who gave no love or respect.

All of which is coherent and potent enough, there's no difficulty believing it. Except for what I now have to tell you: that early in his new career, as Marlon Brando became famous and made real money—$550 a week on *A Streetcar Named Desire,* for example—he simply turned that money, or most of it, over to his dad to invest it. As it happened, the money was lost in cattle schemes, in attempts to reclaim abandoned gold mines, in far-fetched projects where con men fooled his dad.

And the money was gone. Which is not exactly rebelling against authority, even if it strengthens the mood of resentment.

But when the father dies, in 1965, the son reckons that the secretive man had bank accounts the family never found. They may be there still, in small Midwest banks, unclaimed. And in 1994, the son will write about his wish that God might bring that dad back for just eight seconds so he could break his jaw. "I wanted to smash his face and watch him spit out his teeth. I wanted to kick his balls into his throat. I wanted to rip his ears off and eat them in front of him. I wanted to separate his larynx from his body and shove it into his stomach…" The sensitivity is so close to terrible violence.

It's the kind of treatment that, later, might require the delicate re-making of the best Italian mortician respect could command.

HIS MOTHER'S LEAD

When Marlon Brando comes to write his strange, alienated autobiography in the early 1990s, he will give it the subtitle, "Songs My Mother Taught Me." He says he still knows the words to many songs from the '20s and '30s because of her. She was "a delicate, funny woman who loved music and learning." Not that he ever presents her as anything like an ideal opposite to his rough father. Indeed, he says that she "was not much more affectionate than my father." His mother is a drunk; she keeps a "medicine" bottle close at hand that is actually filled with gin. She goes off to saloons on benders, and the young Marlon knows the way the telephone can ring with a request that someone should come downtown to collect a "Dorothy Pennebaker Brando." He recalls, when she sang, the sweet smell of booze on her breath, and he still finds it faintly seductive.

But he does not mention in the autobiography that Dorothy, his mother, was an actress. It's more than likely that he never saw her on stage. She is forced to give it up when the family moves to Evanston, when Marlon is only six. But the family lore has her, for years afterward, lamenting the plight of being the finest American actress not on stage. Perhaps that loss is another thing carrying her toward drink, a grievance that makes her life lonelier or harder to sustain. Or is there, even then, some hint of her son being not just indifferent, but resistant, to her attempt—the very one he will take up? Look at it any way you can contrive, and you cannot forget that

Serious Siblings
In this rather melancholic family portrait from around 1930, the resemblance between Marlon and Jocelyn (top) is striking. Sister Frances eventually married an artist from New York and lived on a farm in Illinois, where Brando occasionally took refuge from the world.

Mother and Son
Brando (at age 8) and his mother
Dorothy had a close, but complex,
relationship.

Marlon Brando takes on his reckless father as a kind of business manager, and simply omits the most important passion in his mother's life.

Dorothy Pennebaker as a young woman is not quite beautiful, but she impresses everyone who sees her. The daughter of a gold and silver prospector who dies when she is only two, she is a blue-eyed blonde with the kind of carved face others will note in her son. Raised in Grand Island, Nebraska, she studies at the University of Nebraska College of Nursing in Omaha. But she gives that up to marry Marlon, who has just enlisted in the Army. She has three children—Jocelyn, Frances and Marlon Jr.

But by the time Marlon Jr. is born, on April 3, 1924, in Omaha, Nebraska, she joins the Omaha Community Playhouse. She is encouraged to audition by a close friend, Harriet Fonda, the older sister of young Henry Fonda. Dorothy or Dodie Brando and Henry or Hank Fonda will be stars of the Community Playhouse. Which suggests that Dodie was more than just a provincial ingenue, a local star. For a few years, she played challenging lead roles in *The Enchanted Cottage*, *Liliom*, *Anna Christie*, *Pygmalion* and *Beyond the Horizon*.

She was good. Not just local reviews say so, but visitors from New York. Otto Kahn, patron of the New York Theatre Guild, encourages her to try Broadway. But days and nights at the theater are measured as absence at home. When Marlon Sr. takes the job that will move them all to Evanston, it is the end of her active theater life. Years later, when she is involved again in something called amateur theatricals (she is unwell), Marlon—a success already in New York—tells her that if she writes a play he will help put it on. But in his own book, he never refers to her having been an actress.

He never seems to have asked her what it was like—no matter that she lived long enough to see *A Streetcar Named Desire*, and to visit the set of *On the Waterfront*.

There's a photograph of that visit. She is fifty-six, but she looks older. She wears an overcoat and a hat (it was such a cold location), and she has a cigarette in her hand. Over the years, she and Marlon Sr. separated a couple of times, and Dorothy had lovers (married men). But those things always ended unhappily, and she went back to Marlon Sr., defeated. That is the look on her face.

IMAGES OF YOUTH

There are pictures of him as a child, a rapturous blond boy called Bud by his parents and sisters. His eyes are set wide apart, his brow is deep and curved, his mouth is already large but delicate, with a slight overhang in the upper lip. He seems sensual but kind, a boy of deep, inarticulate feelings. When he is five, six and seven, the face is open, dreamy (he seems to be looking far away) and you can feel he has his own, dogged slow pace. There is determination and character aplenty, even if he never looks like the smartest kid in the Midwest. But there is something close to a beauty that slips away shyly around the age of eight, and won't come back until his early twenties.

It is not what anyone calls a promising childhood. He does not do well, out of natural lack of ability, but also from a disposition not to please people, or to be ingratiating. He will say in his own book about his life that he hardly remembers words of praise from anyone. Yet that does not fit the collected photo album of his childhood, where we see the mother, patient and attentive, and two older sisters who seem to dote on him. One of the sisters writes on the back of a picture: "Bud—and is he a grand boy! Sweet and funny, idealistic and oh, so young." His book seems blind and deaf to that much fun or pleasure. Perhaps he prefers to nurse pain and anger, and sometimes looks pouty or narrow-eyed as an older boy because hardship doesn't exactly crowd his placid existence. He is proud about being anti-authority, but perhaps he is simply perverse, stubborn, very firmly and calmly set on himself.

In which case, childhood may not matter much: think of it as water off the duck's back when the bird has a rich coat of thick, oily feathers—like armor even.

HENRY FONDA

Contrary to his easygoing screen image, Fonda was difficult and temperamental.

Henry Fonda (1905-82) was born in Grand Island, Nebraska, the descendant of a family of Dutch settlers who had founded the town of Fonda in upstate New York. The family moved to Omaha, where his father worked as a printer. Young Hank was a newspaper writer who studied journalism at the University of Minnesota. In 1925, Brando's mother invited Fonda to try out for a play at the Omaha Community Playhouse. The experience changed his life. Fonda would go on to a major career on stage and screen, getting an Oscar nomination for *The Grapes of Wrath* and winning one for *On Golden Pond*. And he is only one of the strange concentration of actors born or raised in Nebraska: Fred Astaire, Montgomery Clift, Dorothy McGuire, Robert Taylor and Nick Nolte, as well as Brando.

Lonesome Cowboy?
Brando (at age 8 in Evanston) looked ready to round up the bad guys, but the smile hid a growing disdain for authority. In Westerns, Brando would play wronged outlaws (*One-Eyed Jacks*) and irregular regulators (*The Missouri Breaks*).

You can be sorrowful over this Bud's childhood (and that thought plainly occurs to Marlon himself when he has a past to reflect on). But despite several relocations, a belligerent father and a distracted mother; despite doing poorly in school, getting expelled from military academy and never going to college, still, at eighteen or so— when young Americans his age are dying in the war—Marlon Brando is shipped off to New York (unfit for war, but fit for anything else), where he wants to be, without too much family grievance or dispute, and it turns out very well. He is a star at twenty-three, having presented a rare kind of child-bull on the American stage, one that many Americans find both disconcerting and dead attractive. So it works out.

Yes, he moves, or is moved as a kid— from Omaha to Evanston, and then to rural southern California and back to Libertyville, Illinois, thirty miles or so north of Chicago. And the moves may be put down to the waywardness or the instability of his parental situation. But he seems cared for: not just those sisters, but a pony in one picture, cowboy clothes in another, and the overall air of reasonable comfort when many Americans are desperately hard up. Marlon Sr. is earning $15,000 in the mid-1930s—plenty to pay for the move and the local scandals about the mother's alcoholism, and still have a fair standard of living.

Bud is not academic. He flunks kindergarten; his grades are always poor; there is the possibility that he has some kind of dyslexia; he stammers, or mumbles out of uneasiness with words. (Much later in life, some note that he needs to read aloud.) He does a bit of drama in high school, but he is considered difficult: he does not like to say lines the way a strict teacher insists on. He is not reliable. Such things will be reported, in more sophisticated ways, by later directors. Yet the boy is often seen reading quietly on his own, and one of the few teachers he admires or remembers is the one who introduces him to Shakespeare. All his life, people will remark on his urge to get into prolonged, earnest talks about enormous matters.

He reads people, too. In his teenage years, girls especially are captivated by his habit of watching them intently, without talking much. Some say it feels like being mentally undressed; the more discerning seem to see that he is absorbing or studying their very being. And the study shows. He can do weirdly exact acts of mimicry; in drama class, he does a mime of a woman taking a bath—it's so startling that everyone, the girls especially, wonder how he managed to see them!

This is also one of his pranks, a manner of teasing. He loves practical jokes, silly physical acting out, but he is not malicious. And though he is not very good with words, with writing and ideas, he has a knack for practical things, and is very adept at fixing simple household items. Maybe his happiest day ever in school is when he makes a screwdriver and is praised for it.

He goes off on solitary walks and he is much attached to animals—there is a cow it is his job to milk. He loves the cow. He keeps a cat, a dog, raccoons and other pets, and he is inclined to talk to them: is that sentimentality, or the early taste for an audience that won't argue back?

He listens to the radio and at the movies he loves cowboy serials above all, especially Hopalong Cassidy.

He loves drumming. He has a full kit set up in his room and plays along with the great swing bands of his teenage years—Benny Goodman, Gene Krupa, and so on. And he listens to black jazz, too, which is a rarer taste in the Midwest, though it has affected people like Bix Beiderbecke and Hoagy Carmichael before Marlon. He carries drumsticks with him and is a known pest for beating out the rhythm he hears in his head. He has no formal musical training, but jazz is the music for those who depend most upon themselves and the need to utter songs heard in their own heads. He will have gauged by the time he is twenty or so that there are profound rhythms in inarticulacy and its sighs. Girls especially are susceptible to them.

SHATTUCK

Here's an intriguing point: Marlon Brando in 2002 is seventy-eight. Al Pacino is sixty-two. Pacino has made thirty-five films, Brando thirty-nine. What's the point? In part, that Pacino (Brando's heir in *The Godfather*, and one of the greats in the next generation of actors) seems likely to make far more pictures. And Pacino also acts on stage still.

But here's the other point: in just one of Pacino's pictures, he plays a military man—albeit retired, or forced out of uniform by blindness. I am talking about *Scent of a Woman*, his Oscar-winner. Yet Marlon Brando, a professed enemy to authority, and someone expelled

THE DRUMMER

Brando keeps the beat with musician Jack Costanzo in Hollywood, 1955.

In 1945, Brando visited the Katherine Dunham School of Dance in New York. It was a place where most students were black, Haitian or Spanish, and where there was great stress on drumming. He studied conga drumming with the Haitian teacher, and certainly heard a lot about the voodoo associations. Observers noted that Marlon would drum for hours, often chanting, as if in a world of his own. The overall impact was to make him intensely attractive to women at the school, though Marlon seldom let himself make eye contact with them. Years later, in Tahiti, he kept bongo drums in the bathroom and never relieved himself without playing a riff.

from military school, has eight times been a member of the military—and that is not counting *Viva Zapata!*, *Julius Caesar* or *Morituri*, in all of which a kind of armed service is employed.

What should we make of this?

Marlon Brando enters Shattuck Military Academy in Minnesota in September 1941. He is a year older than his peer cadets, because he has had to repeat his sophomore year in high school. It is true that he will be asked to leave the academy, but under uncommon circumstances that also speak to just how good a time he had there. Let's note, too, that he is at Shattuck, sometimes occupying the desk his father had sat in before him, when America is attacked in December 1941.

Some of his letters home are quoted in his autobiography: they are full of the regret that his parents don't write to him much, and there is the steady apology for his grades' not being very good. A boy and a cadet then may have been expected to keep a brave face in letters home. But these letters cannot quite suppress the real enthusiasm he feels. The setting and the Gothic buildings clearly impress him. He seems to like the others guys and to get on. He plays a lot of football, and enjoys it; he makes the drill team; he's in the drum and bugle corps, the orchestra and dance band. "Jesus, I can't wait to see you and tell you some of the Godawful funny things that happen here …"

He is a class character: quick-tempered and violent sometimes but popular, amusing, a bit of a riot. Hating loud intrusive noises, he takes action against the bell in the campus tower and steals the enormous clapper—all 150 pounds of it—and buries it. But life gets better: he reads books he loves—*The Three Musketeers*, *Wuthering Heights* and Shakespeare. He has the best teacher of his school years, a man named Duke Wagner, who introduces him to Shakespeare and encourages him to do a little acting. His parents might have written to him more, but in reading his letters home they had reason to be pleased, to think that the aimless boy was finding himself.

More than fifty years later, in the published autobiography, he sees it differently. He says he wanted to destroy Shattuck because of its stress on uniformity. "I hated authority and did everything I could to defeat it by resisting it, subverting it, tricking it and outmaneuvering it. I would do anything to avoid being treated like a cipher, which is what they aim for when they put you in a military uniform and demand conformity and discipline."

Something happens in his second year. It may be just the accumulation of his pranks, his bad grades and his cutting drill classes. It may be more. There may be some sexual encounter with an adult at the academy. The older man never spells it out.

Unlikely Cadet

Although his letters home suggested enthusiasm for military school, Brando later wrote that he despised the experience. His personal recollections of a sad childhood and youth contradicted the memories of those who knew him.

Home Leave

Brando takes a break from
Hollywood (but not photographers)
for a 1951 visit to his parents at
their farm in Libertyville, Illinois.
Mending the doll (for an unnamed
niece) is Brando's sister Frances.

At the school, the favorite Shakespeare teacher embraces the unruly kid
and tells him he will be heard from—this opinion is given with confidence,
and no one has been so high on Bud Brando before. Once he has left, the
student body bands together to protest his dismissal. And at a military
academy in wartime, the authorities relent: they write to young Brando
offering him the chance to come back for summer school to finish his credits
and then move on. Of course, he tells them where they can go. That wild
one ain't going back.

But then, in later years, he will pretend to be a soldier struggling
with paraplegia (*The Men*); that archetypal soldier who did it his way,
Napoleon (*Desirée*); a pilot who seeks to marry out of his race (*Sayonara*);
a bright blond Nazi who becomes disillusioned with his Reich (*The Young
Lions*); one of history's most famous overthrowers of authority (*Mutiny on
the Bounty*); a homosexual in the army (*Reflections in a Golden Eye*); a
mercenary who falls afoul of his employers (*Burn!*); and a colonel named
Kurtz, perhaps the best soldier of his generation, driven so mad by war in
Vietnam that he goes up the river and turns his command into a grisly
empire (*Apocalypse Now*).

New York
1943–1948

MAELSTROM

Will there ever be a headier time than New York from about 1943 to 1948? That's when Marlon Brando goes from being nineteen to twenty-four. Look at that sleek, smiling, fattening face on the young man. Among all the things you have to notice, and wonder over, one could imagine the caption—"Am I lucky!" Yes, the cry has an exclamation mark, not a question mark. After all, nobody called the show *Oklahoma?* Or the movie *Viva Zapata?*

What a wonderful country where, amid the most extensive war ever fought, Marlon Brando can come to the big city 4F (because of a knee injury from football, and nearsightedness) and be able to take advantage of the absence of so many young men, and be able to grab just about any girl he wants, before appearing on the stage as the embodiment, dripping with Louisiana heat and desire's sweat, of rough young American maleness? Was Stanley Kowalski 4F? Or 4F!?

Brando sees a lot of action; he is a center of activity; and he will become the model of American acting. Don't be shy of the artillery beat in all those "act" words—and remember that Marlon is a drummer! This war is, after all, an American war, nothing like the First World War, where participation came late and served in just a European theater of conflict. Americans can tell the story of World War II from their point of view. And because it is a just war, or a good war, or an unavoidable war, soldiery is heroic, and there are leaders who will become essential political figures—active Americans the country is proud of: Patton, MacArthur, Marshall, Bradley, Eisenhower—pin-up generals beside the map in every boy's room where flags on pins track the slow surge of victory!

The nation is at war; it is regimented. And even if Marlon Brando will become a brooding figure offended by regimentation, in the years after Shattuck he keeps hung on his wall the letter, the petition, in which the cadet force beseeched his return to his proper place as one of the guys.

There is no deeper proof of this energy, this will, this confidence than all the explosions at home that keep up the beat of war. It is between 1943 and 1947 that Jackson Pollock (they will call him an action painter) begins to let paint flow and drip on canvas as if it were a bodily fluid. Similarly, in the thing called "abstract expressionism" the ordinary eye sees explosions of color, form and paint. In Willem de Kooning's pictures, by chance, the color scheme and even the shapes of outburst are strangely akin to the first atomic explosions in New Mexico—and then exported. That is not meant ironically. The atomic bomb has its doubters from the outset, and their case will grow as more is learned about fallout, half-lives and being downwind. But do not doubt how far, in 1945, the big bangs are in harmony with the nation's cocky, energetic sense of supremacy and purpose. America is proud of its bomb—for a moment.

There is a new generation of writers. Saul Bellow's *Dangling Man* appears in 1944. Gore Vidal begins to publish. Truman Capote's first stories appear. And in 1948 Norman Mailer publishes *The Naked and the Dead*—and is actually one of the first people Brando meets in Greenwich Village and chats to, before Norman Mailer is shipped out to the Pacific.

On one kind of stage there will be Tennessee Williams and Arthur Miller. On another, there is *Oklahoma!* itself (premiered in 1943), *Carousel* in 1945 and *Kiss Me Kate* in 1947. In New York, in 1948, Georges Balanchine choreographs *Orpheus* to music by Stravinsky. The Third Symphony of Charles Ives is first played in 1946. Aaron Copland performs "Rodeo" in 1942 and "Appalachian Spring" in 1944. His "Fanfare for the Common Man" is first heard in 1942. In 1949, the movie *On the Town* will summarize so many

Musical Milestone
This whimsical poster for the 1943 musical *Oklahoma!* belied the production's artistic triumph. Its creators, Richard Rodgers and Oscar Hammerstein, introduced hit songs ("Oh, What a Beautiful Mornin' ") and a serious (by Broadway standards) story. Its greatest legacy could be that exclamation point, which changed musical marquees forever.

N. Y. CITY CENTER
LIGHT OPERA COMPANY
JEAN DALRYMPLE, Director
presents

OKLAHOMA!

reasons for feeling on top of the world in New York City.

Of course, I am already past a date in the chronology that needs to include the appearance on the New York stage of Marlon Brando in *A Streetcar Named Desire*. For the headiness of this age or moment is such that a kid, an onlooker, a spectator can go to being not just a great actor, but the embodiment of the idea of acting—to being action!

No, I am not saying that Marlon Brando knew enough to hunt down Franz Kline and Adolph Gottlieb in small New York art galleries. I doubt he could have afforded a ticket to *Oklahoma!* There is no record that he read *Dangling Man* or attended the performances of Ives's Third Symphony. But he was there, in that city and that moment, and he felt he was having a hell of a time.

We do know, that he attends one of the other great explosions that is occurring in New York: the first manifestations of bop (no, it has to be bop!), modern jazz, the hectic, scary, scalding, going-on-for-ever thrust of raw improvisation from the chord changes of some classic song. I am talking about Charlie Parker as well as drummers like Kenny Clarke, Max Roach, Art Blakey, not to mention all the Cuban or South American drummers that crowd out New York in the craze for Latin music.

What happened with bop in '43, '44 and '45 was crucially New York because the music was live. There were great restrictions on record-making during the war (the necessary shellac was in short supply) so the new music and the new black attitude do not break on ears at large until '46 and '47. But Marlon is there in person, and he is discovering his enormous fondness for just about anything of color. He was not musically trained, but no one could miss the rhapsodic daring of this new music, and no one remotely interested in acting, I think, could fail to see how Parker on the alto is a new way of uttering (thus it affects all discourse, including speech). And nothing will be so shocking about Brando the actor as his utterance—the roaring and the mumbling, and above all the sense of someone speaking when he does not know what he is going to say (as opposed to that schooled utterance of classical theatre, in which people have been speaking these speeches for centuries).

If you seek to grasp what was novel, daring and intimate in Brando's acting, listen to Charlie Parker's assertion of a new way of thinking—a kind of breathless rapture, driven by rhythm.

Bird Watching

In songs like "Ornithology," sax player Charlie Parker (nicknamed "Bird") helped invent a new type of jazz that was meant for listening, not dancing. Bebop was intellectual and hip—and it was never very popular with the masses, which was rather the point.

Vagabond Chic

Long before he played biker Johnny in the 1954 film *The Wild One*, Brando had cultivated the disheveled style of the modern noble savage—a primitive genius with nothing to lose.

VAGABOND

Sometimes the most decisive thing an actor does (though it can be destructive, too) is to say, just like a kid trying to dominate play, "It's my game. My story." The young Marlon coming to New York is like that. It is not simply that he takes possession of the plays—the theatrical narratives—in which he finds himself. Rather more, he surveys the space that is the theater as a whole and claims it emotionally as his territory. Not just because he is the best, or the natural center of the story. But because he has an instinct for the passion or the energy that drives the engine. It is force—and it is irresistible.

Put it this way: in *A Streetcar Named Desire* (1947), the household where the Kowalskis, Stella and Stanley, live in New Orleans is invaded by Stella's older sister, Blanche DuBois. Blanche wants space for her nervy privacy; she tries to alter the light and the tone. Stanley reacts like an endangered species, albeit a rogue male. He wants to rip down Blanche's enclosure—he wants her out of there, for it is his place. You can say that a similar battle takes place over the play itself—a struggle to determine who is the central character. And in Brando's great moment in the theater (it will be the only time, for the bored conqueror moves on), he seems bent on overwhelming the pre-existing rules or atmosphere. He wants the stage recognized as his place.

Don't underestimate in this the intense fear that the ordinary, unschooled provincial feels. That is why he makes himself into so deliberately a "vagabond"— as opposed to beginner, student, novice or apprentice. In other words, without experience, he somehow lays claim to a more primitive level of knowledge (or instinct), one that may disarm or daunt people with far more education or sophistication. Indeed, it is like an outcast forced into the allegedly artful intrigue of government, with some innate and fearsome power, a force enough to make "them" an offer they can't refuse, an insolent, violent, dangerous, uncivilized roar that may silence witty and civilized conversation. It has always been a part of Brando, and it has its origins in the American dream that in all the new nation's space and power and opportunity there must be a spark or an explosiveness (that bomb again) to overawe the accumulated discourse of cultural history. Never doubt the awful, little-boy pride in America's most American presidents at sitting on top of that column of fire.

Teacher

Somewhere between Margaret Sullavan and Barbara Stanwyck, Stella Adler nearly made it as an actress. Disappointed, she became one of the great teachers of that art.

The word "vagabond" does occur. It is uttered by Stella Adler, his teacher, the doyenne of that world and moment, a woman surely aware that she may be "making" Marlon Brando, yet fleetingly aware perhaps that, fifty years later, she may be famous or known for having been his teacher.

He is nineteen, she is forty-one. (No wonder, soon enough, Dodie Brando comes to New York to be "with" her wild son—for motherhood may be at issue). Stella Adler is the daughter of Sarah and Jacob Adler, he a great star of the Yiddish theater. In the 1930s, Stella becomes a star player with the Group Theatre. In a way, she is the goddess of that movement, attractive and feminine enough to move Harold Clurman and Lee Strasberg, and to get the attention of fellow actor Elia Kazan. She plays many lead roles; she marries Clurman, who is the intellectual head of the Group; and as an emerging teacher she breaks with Strasberg when she feels that the little tyrant is twisting Stanislavsky's faith in insisting on memory exercises. She visits Paris with Clurman in 1934 and discovers that Stanislavsky now regards acting less as a doctrinally intense, technical journey back into the psyche and more as an imaginative process open to anything that works.

As its name suggests, the Group Theatre believes in political commitment and producing plays with social value in the hard times of depression and spreading fascism. On the other hand, several of the Group actors listen to Hollywood offers—John Garfield; Stella's brother, Luther Adler; Franchot Tone; and the beauty in the band, Frances Farmer. Stella is very attractive and very sexual: she has wild blond hair and an animated, sensual mouth. She does a few small roles in movies herself, but she does not "take." And as soon as Farmer appears, it is plain that Stella is hardly beautiful. No one has to spell it out, but her nose looks a little Jewish. Or a lot. She is empress to her circle, but a little disappointed not to have conquered the rest of the world. She is acclaimed as a brilliant teacher, more direct than her rather wordy husband Harold, as incisive as she is as an actress. And surely such a woman as a teacher, with her own dismay, is ready for

THE GROUP THEATRE

The Group Theatre was founded in 1931 by Cheryl Crawford, Harold Clurman and Lee Strasberg. It was an attempt to establish a permanent company that would perform in New York and which would develop and produce politically committed (or left-wing) plays. The Group broke up in 1940. But in that prior decade it had great successes with *Awake and Sing!* (1935), *Waiting for Lefty* (1935), *Golden Boy* (1937) and *Rocket to the Moon* (1938).

A Group Theatre portrait includes Elia Kazan (far right of front row); Harold Clurman (center, leaning over two women including Frances Farmer on his left); Lee Strasberg (second from right in back row); Lee J. Cobb (with pipe in back row center); and writer Irwin Shaw (sitting in front).

Clifford Odets was its lead playwright, and the company of actors included Luther and Stella Adler, Franchot Tone, John Garfield and Morris Carnovsky, as well as Elia Kazan.

some astonishing untrained force to come along. Still, in the politically correct scheme of things that has teachers maintaining a professional distance, standards and integrity, it is not exactly the done thing to gaze upon a new kid in class and ask "Who's the vagabond?" in quite that intensely hopeful, ardent way.

Of course, in a play, that line and her reading of it might be perfect, a handle on immortality. There's the sign of young Marlon Brando imposing himself. He comes to class in his first day at the New School for Social Research, and before he has said a word he has cast his own drama over the proceedings, and dared the teacher not to be his follower. Can she risk not being a part of it?

PLAYING CHICKEN

When Stella Adler asks "Who's the vagabond?" she refers to the look of the new boy, maybe—his ragged clothes, the worn sneakers, the unshaved face—but she has seen a beauty within already. She is quietly knocked out (though it may seem loud to her). It's the sort of thing girls in the class might get better than the boys. For they feel it themselves, and giggle to hear the catch in their lofty teacher's voice. And already, it seems, Marlon has been through a few of the girls in the class, in the kind of amiable, munching way that bespeaks a hungry boy who has the trick of seeing that any woman in the world is there as his potential provider.

He does a few things in class for Stella. There's the story of an exercise she assigns: the students are chickens, under some immense threat. All the others flop around, squawking and trying to fly, while Marlon finds his spot, digs in and tries to lay his egg while there is still time. Adler is delighted. Perhaps surprised. The ploy is so daring, and yet maybe so true to life—a chicken's life, as observed by a country boy? Maybe it reminds Stella Adler of herself. Marlon becomes not just her favorite. He ventures into her family. She takes him home to meet her mother, her husband and their teenage daughter, Ellen, and Ellen falls for Marlon. But Marlon concentrates on Stella—not the least likely way of getting ahead. He may not be aware of it, but he begins to copy her. Except that "copy" is a calculating word: it suggests a process of observation, analysis and duplication. Whereas, Adler comes to believe that Marlon is so helpless an actor that, left in anyone's company, he begins to become that person, begins to take on their mannerisms, the rhythm of their breathing, their way of speaking. It is a kind of theft, though inspired far more by love than by malice or envy. And for a very attractive woman of a certain age desperately drawn to this kid, it must be both heady and disturbing sometimes. She tells him to stop— and crosses her fingers, no doubt. He can always say that it's not in his power to stop or control the magnetic attraction of resemblance.

So Marlon crosses his fingers. He starts smoking in class, because Stella smokes. She flicks the ash off in a grand, careless, actorly way (a kind of Bette Davis gesture), and he is soon doing the same. She has a way of wearing a peignoir, with little underwear (she is a play begging to be written), and Marlon starts to expose himself. Others notice and suspect cunning. She ignores the masquerade, for to seize on it might lead her into the very tricky task of separating adoration from talent. And not the least part of this impassioned imitation, of course, is its assumption, its acknowledgment, that she is a great actress and a commanding teacher. Who, really, is noticing whom?

Sometimes the confusion is fevered. Marlon hangs around Stella, or she is the hook for his unwashed clothes. One day she is undressing and realizes he is still there with her in the private place, and she says she thinks he

Suave Impression
Brando was an adept impersonator and could assume the mannerisms of anybody after a few minutes of observation. In this charming 1940s photo, he might have been caught unawares and is simply being Brando.

should leave. But he tells her how beautiful she is, and somehow the way actors can be naked together without it really involving or summoning their real persons covers the delicate moment. Has Marlon seen Stella naked, or just the character she is playing, just "Stella Adler," the great lady of New York acting classes. Wouldn't she like to be her real self? Or does an acting teacher have as much of a problem finding that precious ground as, say, a psychoanalyst?

Not that she leaves him untouched. She gets him to talk about himself. She hears the tales of how monstrous and appalling his father is. She witnesses, with his mother in New York, how far the son is horrified by her weakness, the drinking, and by the wounds left in having wanted to be an actress. But are these real syndromes or the delineation of a character Stella has designed for him? Does he truly need to be relieved of that burden, or is he just delighted to have such a sympathetic character offered? He mumbles, for instance—he often cannot, or refuses to, be heard clearly on stage, in class or rehearsal. There are those, like the New School teacher and director Erwin Piscator, ready to give him up on that account. As if he simply lacks the talent, or the professionalism, to be communicative. But Harold Clurman—the explainer, above all, of that era—discovers that Marlon cannot quite give proper utterance because his inner pain is too great to be announced!

Another explanation is left: that Marlon Brando makes a cult of new, perilous, unclear forms of utterance in that they dramatize how far the play is something only in his head, of his doing and making. His game. What's more, there are those who know him who see this act as not so much heartfelt and therapeutic, not so much a belated response to parental pressures, as part of his need to kid and tease and make practical jokes out of everything. How could anyone that strong, that selfish and secure, be so vulnerable to inner hurt?

ELAINE STRITCH

Like Brando's pal Wally Cox, Stritch became successful on TV, as the star of the early '60s series *My Sister Eileen*.

One of the people who observed Brando in those first New York years, with adoration and fear, was Elaine Stritch (two years younger than Marlon), who later became famous as an actress, singer, comedienne and show-stopper in Stephen Sondheim's *Follies*. Brando and Stritch did scenes together in class, and appeared in productions at the New School. She was smitten with him, but never quite succumbed. And she saw a young man terribly torn between a love of acting and a public reluctance to take it seriously. "He was laughing at all of us. I have a memory of him laughing at everything and everybody, like healthy and a little bit crazy and complicated with the no speaking and all that, but adorable."

PLAYING FOR KEEPS

From the start, he is given small roles—as if lead parts were not worthy of him. If that sounds foolish, see how he makes an early habit of having a modest role dominate a show. He does not struggle like most actors; he does not seem to have to work hard. Given the class assignment to be someone or something in a busy department store, he bypasses ordinary thinking and becomes the cash register—static, his tongue going in and out, making grotesque noises. The store becomes the back-up to its cash register. For Piscator, in Gerhart Hauptmann's *Hannele's Way to Heaven*, he is both Jesus Christ and a feeble old schoolteacher. Yet he is less one or both; he is the variation of one to the other—he is change itself, a tour de force, a show of force.

He is, at much the same time, the son enduring Dodie as her alcoholism is intensified by the big city. But who can say whether that is his authentic grief or just another part? These are so many counterbalancing girlfriends, some of whom help Jocelyn and Frances look after the ailing mother. People rally around Marlon; they cling to him; they want him. One day a male friend finds Marlon wearing a brown paper bag on his head with cut-outs for eyes.

"What are you doing?" he says.

"I'm trying to avoid so-and-so," laughs Marlon, naming one of the girls chasing him. To be in hiding, yet so conspicuous; he is dramatizing every stray mood and situation—until drama may become his being.

He gets a part in a big play: in October 1944, aged twenty, he plays the fifteen-year-old Nels, a Norwegian-American boy, in John Van Druten's *I Remember Mama*. He has lost a lot of weight to suggest youth. He is weak in

Mama's Boy

Still taking a backseat to established stars, Marlon looks on as Oscar Homolka pretends to drive, in a scene from *I Remember Mama*. Homolka, a classically trained Austrian actor, can also be seen in the film version of the play. Costar Mady Christians is sitting next to Brando in the back seat.

rehearsal. He is not speaking clearly. There are some ready to fire him, but the author Van Druten insists on his raw ability and says it is something more than the leads possess—Mady Christians and Oscar Homolka. The part seems plain, but Stella Adler predicts that the play will be a hit.

No one is quite ready for Brando's naturalism. Bobby Lewis, another Group Theatre member, goes to the opening and he sees Christians and Homolka acting up an old-fashioned storm in a very stagy work. "Suddenly, in the back, down the stairs comes this kid munching an apple." He has the apple because eating is a realistic way of muddying speech. "Here were these two great professionals emoting, and then this kid who really looked like he lived upstairs in the house. He started to say his lines, and I said to myself 'It's a stagehand. Someone's just wandered onstage, or maybe it's an understudy. The fellow that's supposed to play the part isn't here, and this guy, he's not acting.' "

There you have it, in 1944, the dream that Brando will bring to American theatre arts and to the life of the nation's dream—that maybe you're not acting. It's the question Stella Adler has to ask herself as Brando is there and she's undressing: is it me he wants—could I be that natural?

I Remember Mama is a hit, and in part that's because Brando gets applause at a simple exit line—"Good night, Mama. Good night, Papa" is all he says. Van Druten meant nothing special by it. So Christians and Homolka are stunned on opening night when the play stops at the line. There is applause as the boy

Sentimental Hit

I Remember Mama was based on Kathryn Forbes's book *Mama's Bank Account*—the sentimental story of a closeknit family of Norwegian immigrants in San Francisco. After the play and its followup film came a CBS TV series based on the story, *Mama*, which aired from 1949–1957. It might have ended there, but for a 1974 horror film called *I Dismember Mama*.

I REMEMBER MAMA

THE PLAYBILL

REGISTERED IN U.S. PATENT OFFICE

FOR · THE · MUSIC · BOX

exits. No one can fathom the moment beyond ascribing it to Brando's unprecedented naturalism—of a kind not witnessed before. As the run continues—over 700 performances—Brando begins to add little things: bits of business, a sigh or a look, a word or two, a grunt. No one stops this growth. Van Druten will later include all of Marlon's little things in the published text. Others in the cast, like actress Frances Heflin, see a kind of steady, organic growth in Nels such as they have never anticipated.

This is an actor coming to life, but it is also a rebel kid bored with the long run of the play. He plays games with the props. One night he puts salt in the family coffee. Another night, the coffee pot won't pour. He is deft at these little bits of wicked engineering, though the professional members of the cast come to fear and loathe him. The kid is taking over the show, so that Homolka and Christians can hardly step forth each night with their old confidence. Is this the beginning of directing or acting as an insurrection within a play?

He seems to wash less. His clothes are filthy. He brings his teeming sexual life into the theater.

He gets girls to wait in his dressing room. There are so many of them, so many dark-skinned or Eurasian. They come and they go. When someone asks why he's sticking with the long run when he's so dangerously bored, he says it's to pay the women—and maybe some are those you pay, or have to pay off. One night a hapless visitor enters his dressing room— the door is never locked— and Brando is naked on the floor with Stella Adler. She is not naked, not quite, but there seems no doubt about what is happening right then—or with Ellen Adler the night before. Is this professional exploration, or is it a demon in the theater? Must even Oscar Homolka guard his virtue? And this state occupies him in the winter of 1944–5, the last winter of the war, a kind of epic abandon—with enormous explosions and revealed concentration camps to come in the spring and summer.

ONE OF THE GUYS

He spends time in Provincetown, that odd kingdom at the end of Cape Cod in Massachusetts. Boredom, or is it a natural laziness, needs some rest during the run. There is no question of this boy being consumed by theater, or driven, forced from one part to another. Life in the theater for him, and life in general—the way he means to lead it—has no long runs, no monotony. So young, he puts his own fickle freshness ahead of everything. So he goes off with a girl, Julie Robinson, but later on as he is doing P-town on weekends, keeping company with a lot of that community's homosexuals, he is more often with his drums than with a girl.

Does one need to ask of this constant experimenter whether he had "homosexual experiences?" Later in life, he will say, yes, of course, he has had more or less the usual exercises in bisexuality, as the young actor from New York seems to have been determined to experience every possible variation of love and sex he could find. He was a visitor in Provincetown over a span of a few months, where he at least met Tennessee Williams—they were not quite strangers the next year, '47, on the eve of *Streetcar*. Which is not to say they had special knowledge of each other.

In the nature of such things, he is often with older, more worldly men, wiser men even—something quite apart from his appetite for young,

Theatrical Trio
In his early 1930s work like *Waiting for Lefty* and *Awake and Sing*, playwright Clifford Odets (right, with Stella and Luther Adler in London) promoted group activism. Later plays like *Golden Boy* dealt more with personal social striving.

NAZI DEATH CAMPS

• In April 1945, American troops free 20,000 inmates at the Buchenwald concentration camp, where 50,000 other prisoners, mostly Jews, were exterminated. The death camps confirm the boundless evil of Hitler.

Former Friends?

After filming *On the Waterfront*,
Brando visits his erstwhile director
Elia Kazan (right, with assistant
director Horace Hough) on the set
of *East of Eden*.

dark women. There are some signs that he listens to them, talks about art
and philosophy and solemn things very vaguely perceived in his half-hearted
education, but richly felt. He longs to entertain great ideas. This belated talk is
nothing to rival real education, exactly, yet it shows Marlon's lifelong taste
for keeping some unknown, offbeat guys around—to talk to, or to play the
game of talk with them. He does not have a habit of cultivating challenging
company, but he can handle the wayward wisdom that some misfits or
failures, philosophy bums, have picked up along the way.

Whatever, think of Provincetown as his first withdrawal, the first time he
considers, well, I might not act. At least, not professionally—or laboriously.
For isn't that a very restricted form? So *Truckline Café* comes as some kind of
rescue, though once again it is not a large or dominating role. Not on the
page, anyway. It's another small part. Are people a little scared still of letting
him be what he might be? Or has no one yet cottoned to the idea that this
force of his could be a whole play?

No matter that it is written by Maxwell Anderson, an established success
with *Winterset* and *Abe Lincoln in Illinois. Truckline Café* proves a complete failure.
The play today is not even in print. Approach the Dramatists Play Service in
New York for a photocopy of the typescript and they refer to it as "the Brando
thing." This is fifty-six years later, for a six-minute spot: but that is a measure
of Brando's myth.

The play is to be produced on Broadway by a new partnership of Harold Clurman and Elia Kazan (thus it is a reprise of the lineup at the Group Theatre, which fades away during the war), with Clurman actually directing the play. It is a play for a post-war reality, with a number of lost souls meeting up in "a diner café on the ocean highway between Los Angeles and San Francisco." The place is so close to the ocean that "every few minutes we are conscious of a rush of water by the beach, the breaking of a wave, and then the long drag of the under-tow going out."

The ocean may not quite fit, but in many ways the play is Sam Shepard before his time. In the third act, a young man comes into the café from out of the night, He is Sage MacRae, a veteran, and he has murdered the wife who was unfaithful while he was away during the war. Stella Adler is heard to tell her husband, Clurman, that if he wants to get laid anytime in the near future then Marlon Brando had better be Sage MacRae. No matter that he reads badly, no matter that Kazan is suspicious of Clurman's judgement, the kid gets the part. This means he has to bow out of *I Remember Mama* before its run is ended. That company summons the will to let its rascal joker go, and overnight a Norwegian adolescent becomes ten years older and so much darker.

It shocks Kazan all the more when Brando asks for $500 a week. The producer has reckoned on $125. They settle at $275—this in a cast that also includes Karl Malden and Kevin McCarthy. The kid has an agent, of course, Edie Van Cleve, but he has done so very little yet by most professional standards. And yet he is doing little except exist to get himself into a new play for too much money and a none too vague threat of cuckolding the director. People say that Marlon is really a very nice, quiet, shy, sensitive boy. Which is nice, for the nice quiet, sensitive people. He also has his insolent way of staring men down that hardly sustains the shy talk. He is an actor, and he is a threat.

In rehearsal, Kazan watches Clurman and feels that the play is doomed—or so he says later; he is a very competitive man, even as a partner. As Sage, Brando has one long speech, and in all the run-throughs Clurman is badgering him to let the words be heard, while Brando seems determined to keep them as no more than the mere sounds of pain and protest emitted by the young man.

In the first act of the play, Sage comes back from the war haunted by a story he has heard—that a girl named Tory, an odd name, the name of Sage's wife, has been with another man in a love-nest cabin by the sea. Let it go, others tell him, but he has to know—there is an unduly literary reaching for the idea in this play that young America has been betrayed by war and its aftermath.

The Next Generation
Contemporary playwrights like Sam Shepard (below) take emotional dysfunction into new territory. But Shepard's rambling and volatile blue-collar characters, like Weston in *Curse of the Starving Class* (who cries out for "Ella!"), seem direct descendants of Stanley Kowalski.

Lee Strasberg
Acting teacher Lee Strasberg (seen here in 1961) did not appear in a film until 1974's *Godfather Part II*. Strasberg played gangster Hyman Roth (loosely based on Meyer Lansky), and was nominated for a Best Supporting Actor Oscar.

In the last act, Sage is meant to come into the café from out of the ocean, where he has disposed of his wife. Brando, in preparation, has a cup or two of water tossed in his face. Kazan takes him aside—this is the threat being challenged, a key moment in their careers—saying how about two guys with buckets of water, and Brando running up and down a staircase fast? So he appears drenched and breathless, spilling the sea and violence around him. It is what makes his great speech elemental and out of control:

"When we went into that cabin—when we saw all the things on the wall—just the way I'd been told—and the ocean out there at the same angle—the way I'd been told—then I knew—and I looked at her—and I saw she was guilty. Then I said, 'Is it true?' and she said, 'Yes, it's true, but don't kill me, because I love you and we can be terribly happy.' Then I took out the pistol and shot her. Ten times. Five—and then five. And I carried her out to the ocean. But I wish I hadn't. I wish she were here. We could have been happy together. I'll never have anything now."

There's a bit more, but in a moment Sage turns himself in to a passing policeman. It's a fragment and a life, and it raises an intriguing theoretical question: does the actor—according to Lee Strasberg's way—have to summon up murderousness from his own life, or, as Stella Adler would have it, does he just imagine and invent from the materials of observation as much as memory? Better still: is there any real difference, or any way in which a natural actor does anything but by both approaches, simultaneously, with a lunging vengeance? And is there not something in Brando's attitude to his own life—the violence, the fatalism, the helpless extremism, and the bewilderment—that begins to be Sage, before any words are uttered? In other words, at this cultural moment of *Truckline Café*, Marlon Brando is somehow the battle of beauty and force, sensitivity and violence, that the age is waiting for. In America as a whole, just as in ordinary people, there is great worry over where all the violence of the war will go once aroused. There are profound, academic theories of dark irrational traits in mankind—in man unkind—revealed by World War II.

The speech in *Truckline Café* is not good enough. If Sam Shepard, say, or Elia Kazan, had controlled that scene they might have felt, hold the play, fix on this moment, and see if we can't build from that. Anderson has perceived something, the threat and its pathos, but he cannot deliver it. Still, the world is waiting.

Truckline Café opens on February 27, 1946 and closes after ten performances. And yet…on opening night there is a standing ovation. Then the reviews are terrible. But somehow, everyone is talking about Brando's bit. Other actors hurry to see him before the show closes. At Sardi's one night, Stella Adler calls him a genius. To look at Marlon, and hear other actors talk, you might think that *Truckline Café* is a sensation.

One of his friends, Carlo Fiore, is in the wings at one of the play's performances. He sees the labor and the buckets of water. He also knows that the opening coincides with the disappearance of Marlon's mother on one of her drinking jags. He hears the ovation as the shackled Sage is led off the stage. He thinks he sees an actor at his peak.

Years later—but not really so many, for it will all happen too quickly— after Marlon Brando has made too many poor, wretched movies, Fiore will harken back to the good old days:

" 'I was thinking about *Truckline*,' I said.

" 'I was insane then.'

" 'You could use some of that insanity now,' I said."

CLASS ACTS

Suppose there is a devil in him, as well as the studious explorer of his own insanity, still that leaves room for an earnest, none too bright young man trying to sound mature or responsible, and trying not to be alarmed by the large, fast world he is entering. As he plays in *Truckline Café*, uncertain whether or not it will succeed, he writes to his parents, "You know, the more I hear the lines of the play, the more I am concerned that it is vitally urgent that every one of us do our utmost to arrange our lives in a rigidly self-disciplined pattern with precise direction and foresight in order to exist as a guide for others who are utterly confused and misdirected." He calls it such a necessary play, and so he can sound like twenty-two, or like someone who has not grown up and who can be bewildered by the life and times of 1946. He is still writing to his parents, still trying to impress them or to win their approval.

Not even a failure sets him back. He is seen by Guthrie McClintic, the husband of Katharine Cornell. McClintic is about—yet again—to produce his wife in George Bernard Shaw's *Candida*, and he believes that Brando might be attractive casting as the distracted, not to say anemic, poet, Marchbanks. I say yet again because *Candida* is something McClintic and Cornell have been doing quite regularly since their 1924 production (Cornell is now fifty-three).

FIRST CANNES FESTIVAL

• The first Cannes Film Festival opens on September 20, 1945, in the French Riviera resort town. The festival's 1939 debut was cancelled after Hitler invaded Poland. Billy Wilder's *The Lost Weekend* is among the films shown.

Stagestruck Couple

Actress Katharine Cornell and producer Guthrie McClintic (seen here on the set of the 1945-46 Tennessee Williams play *You Touched Me!*) were Broadway veterans who recognized the power and potential in Brando.

Once before, they chose Orson Welles to be her young man, and so gradually Brando picks up the markers that help define his life.

Playing with Cornell, Sir Cedric Hardwicke and Mildred Natwick, Brando is plunged into a tradition of classical theater—is it too fanciful to hear the clash of those long, open vowels in "Brando" with all the "icks" around him? That "o" at the end of his name is so sensual and womanly; it seems to go with Garbo, Harlow and Monroe soon to come, just as it surely announces a tradition for De Niro, Pacino and DiCaprio. In so many ways the gaping "o" at the end of his name is as much of a warning as a name like "Kowalski"—and notice this: that if names like "Kowalski" had appeared on the American stage before, they signaled immigrants. Whereas Stanley is unmistakably American. That is the brutish thing that so gets on Blanche's nerves—and which makes her seem like the outsider.

In *Candida*, Brando is more scared than he has ever been—all that class tells on him. Nor does he often think to upstage or goose these elders and betters. He is hard put to maintain the educated voice that Marchbanks the poet requires. (Brando knows what few others have picked up on, that he can hardly speak in a fluent, regular way.) And he is playing a character who never gets to control or dominate one moment of the drama. Indeed, there are those who come to the conclusion that Marlon is doing George Bernard Shaw both to prove himself and to broaden his horizons. He is nowhere near crazy or possessed; he could be—as Cornell herself was pleased to announce—a gentle, nice, hard-working boy. Or a Brer Brando lying low.

A Flag Is Born

Brando hoists the flag of Israel (and figuratively beats the drum for Zion) in Ben Hecht's polemically driven play *A Flag Is Born*. It was Brando's first taste of political theater, and it would be many years before he again took up a cause.

This diligence shows no sign of flagging in his next venture: *A Flag Is Born*, a very broad, controversial new play by Ben Hecht in his latest mood of Zionist sincerity, a play about what a good thing a new Israeli state would be. Luther Adler, Stella's brother, directs a cast led by Paul Muni. Marlon plays David, a dedicated Jew who leads the cause against a cynical Britain—in stirring sentiments that the young actor apparently believes in just as devoutly. Yet again he has a moment—a building curtain speech, a tirade of rightness that asks where people were when the six million died, and what they were doing, a speech calculated to make people send checks for Israeli freedom. His energy confounds Paul Muni—once a celebrated actor, as well as a master of character disguise—though Marlon tells everyone how much he is learning from the great man. (Does he notice how quickly a once great actor can become a ham?)

The play opens on September 5, 1946, and it is hot in the news until Ben Hecht goes a little too far. He takes out an advertisement in the New York *Herald Tribune* to celebrate recent Jewish "terrorist" actions against the British Army. Many celebrity supporters flinch, and Brando is left nearly alone with his old hero. Politics is a tricky business if you act on principle alone.

It may be the deserving comeuppance of such a solemn young zealot that he should next encounter Tallulah Bankhead. Tallulah then is forty-three, haggard in her way but crazy for young lovers and the flesh that goes with them. The pretext is a play, *The Eagle Has Two Heads*, written by Jean Cocteau, in which a queen attempts to seduce a young poet. It appeals to her in having a half-hour monologue and in offering her the chance to lay her hands on this hot boy, Brando.

Marlon, as we know, is up for nearly anything in the way of female flesh, so long as it is young and he is in charge. Tallulah (an all-knowing person) likely has heard of Stella Adler's way with the genius and wants some of it herself. It may make her younger. And she, no idiot, no novice, may have humor and wit that could be ample payment for a few rough nights. She appears casually naked before him; he declines to notice. On stage, she makes a meal out of kissing him—combatively, he tries peanuts, garlic and mouthwash.

He is fired, his virtue intact. Helmut Dantine takes over and is slayed by the critics. Which is all very comic and no loss to theater and literature. But Bankhead might have taught Brando so much, and he seems to have an injured innocence once the risk of real education comes in sight. The object of the lesson would be not just sex, or even kindness. Tallulah knows absurdity, knows the real mockeries of class and the necessary duties that beautiful angels must owe to time and mortality. She could prepare Brando for so much. But he elects to remain as a threat to any kind of far-reaching cultural resonance. He queries others—but he is not good at asking. He is the prodigy who has few other futures except to turn into a tyrant.

PRELUDE

And now he does not work for six months. He is so young, so strong; he seems able to work his way through so many of the young women in or attached to Manhattan. He tires easily when work is involved, and even

Some Like It (Not)
As she's not dressed for the stables, it's anybody's guess what Tallulah Bankhead (in *The Eagle Has Two Heads*) has in mind with that riding crop. Alas, she failed to make Marlon her whipping boy.

acting seems like a chore. There are, meanwhile, stories of abortions that some of the women require. In the new, bohemian mood of free love, there is a daft defiance of methods of birth control. Marlon Brando needs to feel free and unencumbered. All of this occurs against an untidy circle of artistically minded young people for whom Brando is already something of a prince. He has a name, a record, and a good deal of money saved up, enough for loans, for abortion fees and to help support his pal Carlo Fiore's drug habit. At this very time, Brando receives a Hollywood offer, for as much as $3,000 a week (a very good sum for a beginner), from Louis B. Mayer, the West Coast boss of Metro-Goldwyn-Mayer. Brando turns it down. The only way this sort of rogue can ever handle Hollywood is with indifference. And here he is more novel or more romantic than most other New York theater actors who are candid about wanting to get into pictures. A great moment is coming in which Brando will tower over such guys with his innocence, his force and his danger.

In the summer of 1946, Tennessee Williams has completed a first draft of *A Streetcar Named Desire.* His previous work, *The Glass Menagerie,* a big hit, with Laurette Taylor in the lead, produced by Eddie Dowling (who also acts in the play) and Louis J. Singer. Williams and his agent, Audrey Wood, are not inclined to use that team again. Indeed, Wood initiates a new production deal, one that will be very controversial. She has heard that Irene Selznick is breaking up with her husband, movie producer David O. Selznick, on account of his gambling, his emotional unsteadiness and his affair with his young contract actress Jennifer Jones. Thus Irene, an authentic Hollywood princess, the younger daughter of Louis B. Mayer, plans to move from Los Angeles to New York. She is hurt and damaged by the end of her marriage, but she is a famously shrewd woman, a very good judge of projects, and rich.

Irene asks for *Streetcar.* She reads it, likes it and sees its power, but she feels it may be too much for someone who has so far produced just one play (Arthur Laurents' *Heartsong*). Then Wood persuades her. It helps that Irene has wealthy backers—like Cary Grant and Jock Whitney, recently her husband's partner in the making of the films *Gone With the Wind* and *Rebecca.*

The Selznicks

David and Irene Selznick had regal Hollywood blood lines—he the son of Russian-immigrant film mogul Lewis J. Selznick, she the daughter of Russian-immigrant film mogul Louis B. Mayer. It was a match made in movie heaven, but it didn't work out.

She will also put up $25,000 of her own, like that, the check now. This is heady stuff for Broadway, and Audrey Wood sweeps Williams into the deal.

But then Williams—a fickle man, to be sure—sees Elia Kazan's production of Arthur Miller's *All My Sons*, and he feels desperate for Kazan's authority on stage. Kazan wants the play, too; he can smell a raw sensation, and he has been building his career on stage and screen. But Selznick is thinking of Joshua Logan as a director. There is a battle for control before Kazan and Selznick agree to work together. The eventual deal makes Irene producer, but Kazan gets twenty per cent of any profits as well as creative control.

Irene has had picture people in mind for Blanche and Stanley—Margaret Sullavan and John Garfield (eleven years older than Marlon). It's hard to believe, but Sullavan gives a poor reading, even though she has a voice that might carry Blanche's perilous poetry, a voice that seems in danger always. But Garfield wants a larger, more ingratiating part, and too rich a deal. So they look elsewhere, and the casting falls into Kazan's lap. In Los Angeles, Hume Cronyn is astutely putting on a version of Williams' one-act play, *Portrait of a Madonna* (which contains the germ for *Streetcar*). He puts his new wife, the English actress Jessica Tandy, in the part—and she wins the support of all. She is cast first, no matter that one day she will turn out to be the flaw in the plans. This seems sensible, for surely *Streetcar* is a play about Blanche DuBois.

Karl Malden and Kim Hunter are cast in the other lead roles, as Mitch and Stella. He has been doing solid work for several years already, and she has been a Selznick contract actress who has also caught the eye of Kazan, a director who has difficulty not getting involved personally with his actresses. So Stanley Kowalski remains—twenty-eight or thirty, a former Army master sergeant, the Polack, "survivor of the Stone Age," as Blanche puts it. For Tennessee Williams, "Since earliest manhood the center of [Stanley's] life has been pleasure with women, the giving and taking of it, not with weak indulgence, dependently, but with the power and pride of a richly feathered male bird among hens."

Reading the play, Marlon Brando gulps and makes the hopeful assertion that he is really not right for this man.

KARL MALDEN

Director Brando gives buddy Karl Malden hands-on pointers for a father-daughter scene during *One-Eyed Jacks*.

That Brando defended the casting of Karl Malden as Dad Longworth in *One-Eyed Jacks* against Stanley Kubrick's feeling that a stronger personality was required is proof of their long friendship—and also of Kubrick's sharper casting instincts. Malden (born in 1913 in Chicago, real name Mladen Sekulovich) first worked with Brando in *Truckline Café*, and then again in both the play and the film of *A Streetcar Named Desire*, and *On the Waterfront*. The two friends have not worked together since *One-Eyed Jacks*. Malden went on to become a stalwart actor on film and in television (where he starred opposite Michael Douglas in the long-running 1970s series *The Streets of San Francisco*). From 1989 to 1993 he was president of the Academy of Motion Picture Arts and Sciences, which hands out the Oscars.

But as yet Stanley is only words on the page—just the indicated route of the brute and the violator.

Burt Lancaster is mentioned for the part (again, eleven years older than Marlon, as well as someone who has served in the war). He would have been pretty good, male enough to have seized the crown of American acting in the late 1940s. Anthony Quinn will later play the part on the road, and some will say there was never a better Stanley. Van Heflin and Edmond O'Brien are mentioned in the small talk of casting. Brando is too young, everyone seems to agree, but Kazan recalls *Truckline Café* and the feeling of a bomb likely to go off. Brando says he is going to say no, but when Kazan talks to him on the phone the actor listens and says yes. And there are hints that Kazan is determined not to take no for an answer. For something is beginning to happen to this strange, precarious play in Kazan's scheming mind.

So Kazan decides that Brando should go see Tennessee Williams. It is like declaring a hunch, setting up a blind date. The playwright is in Provincetown as it happens, and Kazan gives Brando $20 for a train ticket there. Then Marlon intervenes, twists the decisive plan. He spends the money, and instead hitchhikes with one of his girls, Celia Webb. He gets there and finds a house with electrical and plumbing problems. Thus, in his own way, he deals with these material obstacles—he may even root out the accumulated detritus in handfuls—so that the helpless artistic set (if that is how you want to see it) is impressed by the young man's blunt practicalities.

Then Brando reads some scenes from the play, with Tennessee doing Blanche. The writer is captivated. They talk, and then the playwright calls New York, jubilant at having found his Stanley— "by far the best reading I have ever heard," he declares. Tennessee likes the way Brando keeps it a non-Hollywood cast, and he notices something about his own play: "It had not occurred to me before what an excellent value would come through casting a very young actor in this part. It humanizes the character of Stanley in that it becomes the brutality or callousness of youth rather than a vicious older man."

But that is hardly what will make for thirty minutes of applause when the play opens a few months later, December 3, 1947, at the Ethel Barrymore Theatre in New York.

Tennessee Williams
Playwright Tennessee Williams (1911-83) was the ideal match for Brando's violent beauty. His plays typically placed striving characters in vulgar situations that destroyed their illusions. After *Streetcar*, Williams wrote other major works like *The Rose Tattoo* (1951), *Cat on a Hot Tin Roof* (1954) and *Sweet Bird of Youth* (1959).

Good Chemistry
Tennessee Williams (without tie, or shirt) gets a laugh out of Brando on the set of the 1959 film *The Fugitive Kind*. At their first meeting, Williams instantly recognized that Brando should play Stanley Kowalski.

Fame
1947—1949

BRUTE FORCE

And so, at last, step right up for that very celebrated if now rather venerable transport, *A Streetcar Named Desire*. A great play? The greatest of our age, some have said, so filled with reverence they cannot see that this vehicle has been making its rhetorical, fussy, grinding journey for sixty years now. So do not expect me to fall completely for the Tennessee Williams play—not if you want to feel the heat of Marlon Brando in it.

Of course, somewhere or other, *Streetcar* runs every night: it invites revivals with grand stars of yesterday as much as it encourages the cautious adventures of amateurs—for while it is supposed to be daring, dangerous and sexually innovative, nothing happens and nothing is said to frighten away any surviving members of that genteel audience, the spinster or unattached schoolteachers from the provinces, those kind of real-life DuBois characters. When I say that artistes like Ann-Margret and Claire Bloom have had their radiant successes in it in recent times you can see that just about anyone with a certain air of the faded rose can get away with it—and will be drawn to it. For Blanche DuBois is the sort of part those actresses are supposed to do. It flatters their literary aspirations just as it shines a kind light on their glamour and their ladylike eroticism. If you're of that mind you can even point to the "range" of Blanche—the famous "nymphomania" (an artistic condition akin to poise in a lady) and then the madness.

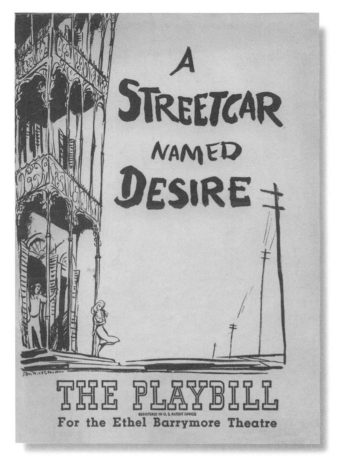

A STREETCAR NAMED DESIRE

THE PLAYBILL
REGISTERED IN U. S. PATENT OFFICE
For the Ethel Barrymore Theatre

End of an Era

The poetic realism of *Streetcar* (as suggested by the original program cover) was short-lived on Broadway. By the 1950s, competition from television, and escalating production costs, brought a shift to more accessible shows, like *Guys and Dolls* and *West Side Story*. Serious plays shifted to smaller, off-Broadway theatres.

Ah yes, the madness. Which means, by the way, some high-strung nature all too easily played upon by unfortunate circumstances— and not the petty, blind, selfish idiocy that is prepared to impose herself on her sister and brother-in-law (in a two-room apartment, and a dump—what a pretty dump!) from May to September, no less. Imagine yourself Stella and Stanley (plus Stella is pregnant!) and ask whether there is or ought to be any way to get past the self-centered stupidity of Miss Blanche DuBois.

Oh, but she is sensitive? And no, she is certainly not accustomed to being treated like this. But, after all, we are on Stanley's side —and so was that first production at the Ethel Barrymore.

For this debut production is a real revolution, the usurpation, even betrayal, of the play. When *Streetcar* is revived, good, solid actors often get to play Stanley. But the production is never known or promoted as Stanley's. It belongs to the star actress. All of which is exactly appropriate—Stanley Kowalski is off the stage a lot of the time. He waits while we have to sit through Blanche's godforsaken attempt at romance with Mitch, surely one of the most pathetic and numbing passages in celebrated modern theater as Mitch is meant to weigh Blanche's cockamamie fabrication of life against the obdurate rigor of his unseen mother! (Mitch's mother is one of those figures in literature I do not want to have to think about!)

Brando takes advantage of these longueurs by having pals in so he can box with them in the theater basement. And one night he comes back to rape Blanche with a broken nose so that he is bleeding all over her. Some playwrights would have seized on that accident and written it in as the perfect payoff to that opening scene where Stanley tosses Stella a white package—staining red—of fresh meat from the butcher.

I know, you are asking whether in those Mitch moments (or the Stella-Blanche duets—they go on and on, no matter that the sisterhood is so implausible) doesn't Marlon have some of his girls in backstage so that he can briefly bed them? Well, I'm glad you ask. Because the answer is no: for artistic reasons (always the best), he wants to be sure of keeping his erection all through the show.

As the rehearsals proceed in the fall of 1947, there is a day when Elia Kazan calls the cast together and says that this is an unusual venture in that everyone must try to adapt to the odd way in which Marlon works. Odd? Well, yes, in that he is likely to be silent, withdrawn, inarticulate, not quite there at first, and even for a good long while, hardly meshing in adequately, or decently, with the others trying to find their way. Remember how Marlon's was the final casting, and notice that Blanche's lines outnumber Stanley's by more than six to one—to say nothing of the way her talk has the "magic" and the alleged "poetry" while he is as raw as the meat he brings home. Then reflect on the production in which that supporting actor is made the center of attention, the bad boy who has to be appeased.

This pressure comes from Kazan and his own need to make a more heterosexual show than Williams has provided. Now, from time to time, in print, Kazan pays lip service to Williams' poetry. But if you read any of Kazan's novels (and they have dated quicker than this play), you'll know his own ear is for language that Stanley might have written after night school (or prison). It's not that Kazan is insensitive: few men are more anxious about themselves, about sex and getting it, and about being in the right. Indeed, those things are vital to Kazan the director on stage or screen, and they begin to account for the curious redirecting (or misdirection) of *A Streetcar Named Desire*.

Nor can I simply write this trick off to Kazan's horny needs. He reads the play; he is a lethal reader of a play and a cruel detector of vulnerability. He sees the dishonesty in Blanche, the airs and mannerisms, and knows how far they mask real tragedy. He picks up on, and feels distaste for, the none-too-buried

Street **Fashions**

Streetcar influenced everything from t-shirt styles (the tighter the better) to production design. The play's designer, Jo Mielziner, created an artfully seedy tenement that seemed both down-to-earth and otherworldly. Reading from left to right, Marlon Brando, Kim Stanley, Nick Dennis, Rudy Bond, Jessica Tandy, Karl Malden.

way in which, for Tennessee, Blanche is your poetical gay southerner itching to be ravished by the rough trade called Stanley. But Kazan is far too macho to identify with that comfortably. And so he rather leaves Blanche alone: Hume Cronyn will protest as decently as he can that Jessica Tandy needs more help. But Kazan says he trusts her in the technical sense—what a diminution of her role that is. He has to work more with the passionate but inchoate Brando.

That work has begun in the casting. Marlon is younger and more beautiful than Stanley should be. Look at the pictures—he is more beautiful than Jessica Tandy! And then, enormous trouble is taken with Brando's look. Jeans were common before 1947, but jean authorities will tell you that they change that December. With costume designer Lucinda Ballard, Kazan and Brando search out jeans that will fit like tights. They are cut and re-cut, laundered and re-laundered, to be sheer, form-fitting. In being fitted, Marlon discovers his own "genius" to go with these jeans. He is delighted with them—and he knows they should be worn without underwear.

Brando finds T-shirts, cut high enough on the arm to show muscle—he is also working out to be in the best shape of his life. The clothes are soiled so that the tightness feels impacted, or armored. In addition, he has vividly colored bowling jackets and the infamous silk pajamas for his wedding night. His own blond hair is dyed brown. Then, and only then, is the play allowed to dwell on his furious, pent-up naturalism—call it animal intensity or presence, call it the Method, or upstaging, like Marlon sometimes scratching and yawning like a naughty monkey as Tallulah Bankhead goes through yards of Cocteau's poetry.

There's an odd reminder: Marlon virtually runs away from the rabid sexual predation of Bankhead. Yet Stanley will surely take Blanche—"We've had this date with each other from the beginning!" he tells her, before he picks her up and carries her to bed (like Rhett Butler with Scarlett O'Hara?). Because Blanche is afraid of him, and is foolish enough to try to live in his cage. Neither Kazan nor Williams, I think, can handle a scene in which Blanche seduces Stanley—though she is a nympho, isn't she, and she is theoretically supposed to be in possession of a greater literary wisdom than her possessor. Today, if we wanted to break the old chestnut open again and have it live, it would be Blanche who takes Stanley and teaches him varieties of sexual behavior that he might find as dirty as they are eye-opening. That is why he would have to murder her—he would be too astonished (too threatened) for her to survive.

That might work, yet it would need a Blanche with all the sardonic insights of an old sexpot ham like Bankhead—a woman who might scorn her own lines. Surely, today, no one can really say "I have always relied upon the kindness of strangers" straight—it has to have the clatter of camp laughter coming in behind it. And Blanche—here is Williams's real truth—

needs to be played by a gay man. The femininity is a performance, or a routine, not nature. That's when or how the threat "she" represents to Stanley becomes so much more than having to share a cramped apartment.

Those hints are there in the text, and I'm sure they played at the Ethel Barrymore in 1947. The astonished reaction to the night must contain so many kinds and levels of surprise. There is the downfall of educated refinement that is Blanche DuBois; there is the nymphomaniac, and the delicate scene where she nearly takes the young man trying to sell *The Evening Star*. There is the melodrama, finally, of some imminent asylum, and Blanche as a broken inmate.

Then there are the Kowalskis. Over the years, Stella has come to be seen as the pivot of the action: Blanche and Stanley fight for her soul or allegiance—and Stanley wins because of marriage and the baby, but also because of rough ordinariness and the body he has. Was Stella ever really Blanche's sister? Stella is not put off by the hard life in New Orleans. Plainly, she craves and has been matured by regular sex with Stanley. Kazan sometimes spoke of "this ordinary young couple" getting on after the war, doing it the American way—which seems to entail disdain for all or most of Blanche's finer worldview (even if she were more supple, more intelligent and more amusing). I don't think it's salacious gossip to add that Brando and Kazan are both, during the production, the lovers of Kim Hunter, their Stella.

The audience sees and feels that very American bond: Stanley's famous cry, "Stella!" the moan of the lonesome beast, and her half-reluctant, half-helpless yielding to it, are part of folklore now. Stella is sane, sexy, wholesome and the future. And she cannot quite condemn the brutality or the violence in her Stanley (even if that means refusing to believe in something we have nearly witnessed the rape). Indeed, she is moved by the force in Stanley, and it is among other things a kind of awed tribute to the young maleness back from the war—the victor, yet maybe in some ways as violent as the defeated enemy.

So Stella is OK, while Stanley is the first juvenile delinquent in American culture, the first kid who wants his space, his meat and his bowling, and the right to be misunderstood. Of course, that right may be a tyranny in the making; it is a "right" that requires ironic quotation marks. But in 1947

The Idea of Rape
Brando and Jessica Tandy in the central confrontation from *A Streetcar Named Desire*—the brute meets the lady, reality wakes the dreamer.

Jean Cocteau
"Marlon is the only man who can make noise without disturbing anybody," said French poet and artist Jean Cocteau (posing in 1956, in the uniform of the Académie Française).

Jessica Tandy

Jessica Tandy had played many supporting parts in films before she became a Broadway star in *Streetcar*. After she lost the film role to Vivien Leigh, her movie career lapsed. But later in life she blossomed onscreen, winning the Actress Oscar for *Driving Miss Daisy* (1989). She died in 1994.

India's Independence

• At midnight on August 15, 1947, Britain relinquishes control of India. The former colony is split into two nations, Hindu-dominated India and Muslim-controlled Pakistan. But the momentous occasion is marred by violence between religious factions.

it speaks for the magnetism of a new kind of American—classless, without ethnic qualification, powerful, handsome, none too bright, and threatening.

You can still feel the thrill, and the beautiful young virtue, when he turns on Blanche with "What I am is a one-hundred-per-cent American, born and raised in the greatest country on earth and proud as hell of it, so don't ever call me a Polack." That's the new America (even if it sounds clichéd and forbidding now, a step towards fascism), and Marlon Brando is one of its first voices—so beautiful, so dangerous, and so much of a new icon to gay and straight alike, even if they are still standing in each other's dark, as well as side by side, in 1947.

So Elia Kazan, like a man exerting a special force in some gadget or widget, twists the play into extra life and meaning. He deserves praise and blame for that, as well as Tennessee Williams's thanks for the play's long life. But it is as if Kazan would have hardly dreamed of doing it all, but for Marlon. The waves of applause cover everyone. Jessica Tandy is said to be very good. But Marlon Brando, in a role six times smaller than hers, is the sensation.

TALK OF THE TOWN

What the hell is an actor to do? Everyone says he "is" Stanley Kowalski and "stunning," or "unprecedented" or "great." With *Streetcar*, all the cast are praised in the reviews, and Jessica Tandy wins a Tony, but the audience's first impulse for coming is to see Brando. He is also far less experienced than Tandy, far less accustomed to soaking up the praise for being someone else, using it for himself, and yet also getting ready to be someone else—another character still. So do not be amazed if successful actors sometimes find themselves unhappier than the failures. Failures have much more stable lives.

The $550 a week Marlon Brando is earning permits so much—to take girls out, to possess a motorbike for nocturnal rides, to be a lordly patron with friends and to go to an analyst, a Freudian named Bela Mittelmann. Brando will complain that his practitioner is cold, but people like Elia Kazan note only that Mittelmann is a star-loving sham, a man who wants free theater tickets, and who is probably as good as Brando needs or deserves, in that the young actor only wants someone to listen to him, and not a full-blooded process of analysis. For that, Brando is too fickle, too egotistical, too playful, too immature. So the talk of hurt is easier than any real sorting out.

The struggle with Jessica Tandy is not attractive, yet it is so plainly set up: she is older, English, she has played with Olivier and Gielgud in her time;

she is driven to and from the theater by a chauffeured car; and she likes to have Blanche in her control—to be consistent and professional—as well as to be the center of the drama. Yet she soon learns that the bored Brando (or is it the stirring of Stanley?) is inclined to make faces at her, to get up to antics as she emotes, and—here's the real pain—the audience goes along with such upstaging because it is so close to the way Kazan has directed Stanley's humiliation of Blanche. In that odd overlap, there is every danger of a young, cocksure, foolish actor believing that he can take a show over, be its author as well as the star attraction.

The publicity machine turns to him, naturally, and he resists. He becomes an early embodiment of the reckless kid genius likely to say anything in an interview—a devotee of the idea that you can lie to protect yourself. He does not see how far that duplicity only traps him into a shattered history that becomes all the more appealing to magazine editors—as it does to himself—in that it seems to offer a warren of hiding places, a labyrinth without a center. Yet a day may come when his own blithe evasions amount to something close to the loss of identity.

Marlon Brando cannot complain: his father now calls him "Marlon" instead of "Bud"; his mother tries to get help from Alcoholics Anonymous— these are gestures of fondness and respect. He likes to tell some people the pain his parents have given him over the years, but Marlon often impresses the same people as someone who seldom detects unhappiness in other people. He prefers his own, no matter that he is one of the luckiest twenty-four-year-olds anyone knows, the most famous stud in town, the hot new actor, the inventor of a new kind of groupie behavior— the one that will become most celebrated a few years later with the breakthrough of rock and roll. Above all, he is worshiped uncritically by most levels of New York society.

He is still a kid flirting with bisexuality: there are guys around him—notably Sandy Campbell, from the rich set—who are there to make a handsome circle and to teach him some of the higher things of life. Not that any of them ever interfere with the horde of girls, but you only knock off the girls, and it is plain already that sometimes with the guys Marlon Brando entertains vague but loftier aspirations. This mood surely helps explain the growth of the Actors Studio, which also opens in 1947, and which has Marlon Brando as its first young model. The method is more Kazan than Stanislavsky; but it is also a lifestyle training under the name of acting classes. John Garfield attends the opening meeting, a Hollywood actor who retains radical links with New York. But Garfield is physically less impressive, a little bit the gutter kid,

John Garfield

In some ways, John Garfield (on the set of the 1939 film *They Made Me a Criminal*) was Brando before there was Brando. He had grown up on the streets of the Bronx, where he was a gang member, and his unconventional looks found him typecast as a surly tough in Hollywood.

THE ACTORS STUDIO

The Actors Studio was founded in 1947 by Cheryl Crawford, Elia Kazan and Robert Lewis as a workshop for actors—membership by invitation only. A year later, the leadership was augmented by Lee Strasberg, who became the Studio's dominant figure, and the strictest adherent to the system, or method, of the Russian director and teacher, Konstantin Stanislavsky, who encouraged actors find inner

1954: a day at the New York Actor's Studio and a front row of Michael V. Gazzo, Susan Strasberg and her father Lee, the teacher, who is doing most of the acting.

justification for their roles, in the memory of the senses. As such, the Studio was the home of what was called Method acting. The Studio exists still, but is best known today for James Lipton's ingratiating interviews with stars (where the method is all flattery).

and he does not have Brando's extreme romantic air—that reaching out that persuades some people that his Stanley Kowalski might be . . . an artist?

There's no need to be mocking, but Marlon Brando at this time will occasionally admit to writers that perhaps he could become an author. Really? they say. What have you written? And he admits, so far, just diaries and letters. Such stories become part of the legend of Marlon Brando, and it is left up to him to decide whether or not he is lying, or posing, when he utters the rather vacuous hope. But at the Studio, he does a few exercises, and he quietly digests notes and criticisms: one that is remembered is Robert Sherwood's 1931 play *Reunion in Vienna*, where he plays a Hapsburg duke, as far from Stanley as he can get, but where he again subjects the woman opposite him to a kind of rape.

As *Streetcar* closes, the level of practical jokes in the company builds along with Marlon's harassing of Tandy. She has to listen to the opinion of Karl Malden that Brando could be very bored, very weary, very irresponsible, his mind a blank (he is not always trying), yet somehow he is always true, while she is correct and predictable. But as the replacement cast comes in (Anthony Quinn and Uta Hagen), after playing on the road, Harold Clurman for one notes that Quinn already restores the balance of the play as written. The feeling dawns that "we" shall never again see *Streetcar* as Brando did it. He is and was so extraordinary that an interpretation dies away with his boredom. What will he do? He has refused all other offers, including an early attempt to mount a movie called *Rebel Without a Cause*, the material that will help establish James Dean just a few years later. There is a treatment by Peter Viertel, and Sam Wanamaker is ready to play the psychiatrist. But then Warner Brothers loses interest. Brando is not sold on the movies, but he lets it be known that enough money might get him. He is still searching for some guiding principle. Meanwhile, he goes to Paris.

INTERMISSION

Everyone urges young, talented people to "get away," to see the larger world, and Marlon Brando has not yet left the American mainland. He is from the middle of the vastness, and he is far from educated. Indeed, even in his recent and sudden professional success, there is every hint that "education" has less to do with his work than instinct. Critics and friends alike tell him that he seems to be in magical contact with honesty. Dangerous advice, for it seems to say to the actor that maybe he will find more drama—more plays, even—within himself. And thus, the heady urge to do without that famous education which is the province of dry, old failures who cannot do the things themselves. Well, maybe, yet no one has so far called Elia Kazan or

First Tango in Paris
When Brando first arrived in Paris in 1949, the city's film industry was gradually recovering from the war. Many top filmmakers, like Max Ophuls and René Clair, had fled to Hollywood. But new directors, like Henri-Georges Clouzot, were exploring the *film noir* style.

Tennessee Williams dry or old. They are men of ideas—and it may be alleged eventually that both of them are the victims of sentimentality, of betrayed talent, or lost direction. But they can wake up any day with the vague shape of a play in mind. Whereas the actor's mind is simply energy, and its greed to find behaviors to imitate. Unless, of course, the actor is tempted to believe in his own magic.

And why should Marlon Brando fall for that one? Well, only because, without ever taking much care of himself, he looks adorable and Adonis-like; because he is young, rich, famous and revered; and because, seemingly, half the young female population of New York reckons he is uncanny, or inspired, or sublime, or magical with sex, while the other half is determined to find out whether such myths are reliable. A time will come, with *Last Tango in Paris* more than twenty years later, when an idea no more nor less than the shape of sex, its transcendence and its own tragedy, will possess Marlon Brando. It is a moment when he will reveal how many other sides of manhood or personality have not been pursued. And it will place him in Paris.

In Paris, in 1949, that lack of pursuit begins to be palpable. The young Brando is very moved, or tempted, by what he feels. This is France only a few years after a terrible war, rife with betrayed ideals, but still the country is reclaiming itself. There is a ferment of ideas—Sartre, de Beauvoir, Camus. There is a young generation coming filled with the urge to reappraise and revivify the nature of film. There are American expatriates again—James Baldwin, Richard Wright, as well as jazz musicians sickened by the racism at home, and soon the first refugees from America's ridiculous fears of Communists in all those dull places like Nebraska, under the bed, or Washington, D.C.

Brando is a bum in Paris. He lives very simply in deadbeat hotels with not much more than Stanley Kowalski's clothes to wear. But he meets Baldwin, seduces the singer Juliette Greco, and sits down with the seasoned movie director Claude Autant-Lara to consider whether he will play Julien Sorel in a screen adaptation of Stendhal's *La Rouge et le noir*. Does he read that great book? Does he know, or care about, French history? The likely answer is "a little…if you go slowly," which can carry the young American from ordering a meal to getting into bed with an aristocrat prepared to test how far Stanley Kowalski can amaze her.

He considers giving up all he has so far—the life of an actor, or rather the career, the big money. He could wander, drift, from one party or weekend to the next. His American money will go a long way. He can see places, knock off places—the young American traveler finds ways of ticking Orléans, Poitiers, Cannes or Arles off the list just as surely as he knows he's had this girl, and that one, and the one in the corner. In other words, he doesn't linger for relationships, or a searching inquiry into all that Arles means for our history—from Rome to Vincent Van Gogh. He's a rolling stone—he always was, years before Mick and Keith—and when you see those wrinkled, ravaged lizard kids still touring you can realize how little education ever

BERLIN AIRLIFT

The Soviet blockade of West Berlin ends on May 12, 1949 after a tense year in which Russian troops prevented all travel to and from West Germany along the Autobahn. During the blockade, the city's 2.5 million residents were sustained by a massive Allied airlift.

Place Pigalle
Paris nightlife in the late 1940s centered around the Place Pigalle, where a strip of jazz clubs and music halls clustered in the shadow of Montmartre.

really got to them. Marlon's like that in that most people he meets have heard of him first. You get the cream like that, maybe, but there's so much more education in sour milk or going hungry.

Is this too harsh? Too severe on a sweet, harmless kid—too much to ask of mere talent? Well, sure, and it's hindsight awareness. But it's also a way of asking you, the reader, why on earth you are so impressed with actors?

CHRISTIAN MARQUAND

Marquand, said a friend, was "able to speak to any girl and bring Marlon that girl if he wanted her."

The French actor Christian Marquand, was born in Marseilles in 1927, of Spanish and Arab descent. Marquand had already made a few films when he met Brando and he was briefly a star in the late 1950s—with Brigitte Bardot in *And God Created Woman*, with Françoise Arnoul in *When the Devil Drives*, and with Maria Schell in *Une Vie*. He directed occasionally, but his career dwindled. Still, nothing detracted from his friendship with Brando, and it is possible that Brando's word got him the role of the French plantation owner in *Apocalypse Now*. That role was cut from the original film, but restored in *Apocalypse Now Redux*. By then, however, Marquand was dead, a victim of Alzheimers' dementia.

Is it that once they've flirted with your fantasies they are required to be important—or hallowed? What is it that's so crushing in this constant age of acting (thanks to film and television), to recognize how empty the great actors may be? I think it is the last chance to insist that there is or could be something more to life, something entirely inward. A very uncomfortable feeling.

Marlon Brando knows that uneasiness. The struggle is there in Paris in his uncertainty whether to slip away, to give it all up—or whether to take on the greatest citadels of acting, art and civilization. To play Hamlet forever? Him with his helpless loathing of anything past the tenth performance? If only acting could…could be like life! With the grand intensity of the process somehow never quite repeated. Do you see how a natural actor would sooner consume lots of women than get into a serious relationship with any one of them? It isn't just the sex—it's the use of energy and the religious retention of freshness. It's what he'd likely call "being alive."

He is a hit in Paris, of course: he doesn't really learn French, but he has a swell knack for imitating it. He can sit at the table in a circle of French and make the sounds—people feel he is "with" them. It is even suggested that he might play Stanley in the French production of *Streetcar*—with the actress known as Arletty playing Blanche—by learning the translated text phonetically! This is put to him by Hervé and Gérard Mille, new friends who own the French rights to the play. They are homosexuals, too, and Brando spends so much time with them that the old stories about sexual exploration arise.

And maybe so. The abiding friendships for Brando are so often male. In Paris, people like Wally Cox (a friend since grade school) and Carlo Fiore are quickly replaced by the young actors Christian Marquand and Daniel Gélin, and the director Roger Vadim. Yes, Brando meets Brigitte Bardot. He meets

Cocteau, too, who is thrilled to stand like a pretzel beside the American beef of such an animal. Those ties will last over the decades, rather better than any friendships with American actors. Brando will name a son after Christian Marquand, and he is surely affected by the greater sense of ordinary, rough reality in French men and artists. He feels more at ease in Paris.

He goes into the countryside and into Italy. Years before he has heard of the Corleones, he even goes as far as Sicily and its burning countryside. One day there, he subsides amid the grass and the wild flowers and says he feels happier now than he has ever felt. Once upon a time (if you like) a great young actor, already famous, just vanished. No one ever saw him again. But then, years later, a figure came out of Sicily, likely to rule the world. And some said he resembled the lost actor. Once upon a time—if you like. But actors do not really choose. They wait for choices to descend on them, like bees on the flowers.

Brigitte Bardot
"There are no nude films, only good or bad movies," said famously nude French actress Brigitte Bardot. Like Brando, whom she met in 1949, Bardot later found refuge in warmer climes and personal causes—in her case, the south of France and animal welfare.

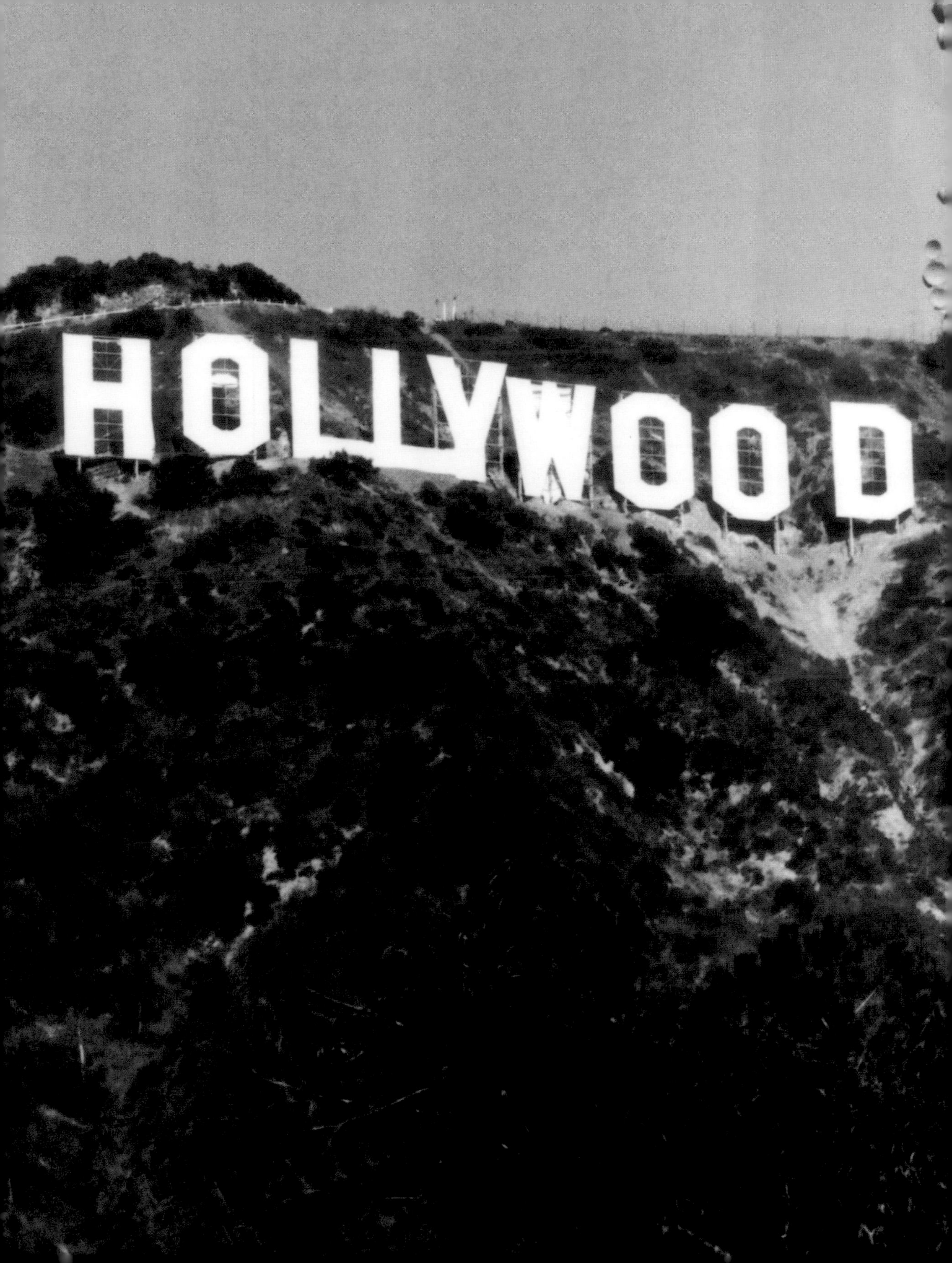
HOLLYWOOD

Hollywood
1949–1958

MEN WORKING

After *Streetcar,* few doubt that Marlon Brando will go to Hollywood eventually. Though the stage beckons, he has discovered his own aversion to long runs. Like many young men, he is sufficiently lazy and interested in money to consider the other way of acting. Not that he seems greedy. He has turned down richer offers, and it is plain that he has an immense suspicion of Hollywood. His first film is a deliberate departure from set or safe norm, a project that proclaims its own courage and independence. And it is the beginning of a career in which Marlon Brando prefers to make pictures that are hardly a part of Hollywood. That sounds grand and resolute. Yet he ends up living in Los Angeles, a place he loathes.

The Men is the kind of picture that Hollywood does not make in 1949: it is a portrait of young men destroyed but not killed by war—of paralyzed survivors, the wheelchair brigade. It could not be better intentioned. Even if the film now seems simple-minded and stilted, Brando remains very powerful in it. No wonder his immediate reputation is enhanced. How striking it must be in 1950, when it is released, that he is again a violent young man returned from the war, but someone in whom the comfortable conventions of service and heroism have turned ugly and dangerous. *The Men* does not mean to be social criticism, beyond asking us to be more sympathetic toward paraplegics, but Brando's character is filled with rage, frustration and hostility.

FRED ZINNEMANN

The director of *The Men* had much to offer the young Brando. Famous for his quiet, sympathetic way with actors, Fred Zinnemann was born in Vienna in 1907. He came to America in 1929 and slowly made his way up to be a director of low-budget B pictures. But in 1949, he made the brilliant *Act of Violence*—in which the wounded Robert Ryan returns from the war in search of a cowardly but much decorated officer,

Zinneman, with Brando and Montgomery Clift on the set of *From Here to Eternity*, sought advice from Elia Kazan on directing Brando. "Don't do anything," replied Kazan.

Van Heflin. Zinnemann worked hard with Brando and always regretted that he never had another chance to direct him. In later years, Zinnemann directed *High Noon*, *From Here to Eternity*, *The Nun's Story*, *A Man for All Seasons*, *The Day of the Jackal* and *Julia*.

He speaks to that widespread postwar dismay about the irrational, antisocial force that may have been released in soldiers. What is most intriguing now in the very limited picture is to see how that force might have been exploited better.

The Men is written by Carl Foreman, produced by Stanley Kramer and directed by Fred Zinnemann, all of whom reckon they are making a daring and difficult film outside the mainstream. The hero, Ken Wilochek (another "Polack"), known as "Bud," is seen first leading a strangely unreal platoon advance. This is Brando in a helmet with a gun, looking as moody as Elvis Presley, posing too much. He is shot down, and will soon learn that he will never have movement below the waist again. He goes to a hospital for paraplegics, where Everett Sloane is the tough doctor in charge, and he battles through anger, denial, self-pity and so on, moves from a lone room to an open ward where he can become part of the sardonic camaraderie, and makes himself meek enough to marry his very sweet sweetheart (played by Teresa Wright).

The earnest social message on behalf of these forgotten men is not to be denied, especially at a time when medical science had learned enough to keep "wrecks" alive without knowing how to handle them. And Brando is a very ripe wounded hero—charged with inexpressible feelings, thunderously real, and easily carrying the film toward the pent-up inner state that, truly, it is afraid of. After all, the begging question in the scenario is will Ken be able to make love with his new wife? Yet the picture cannot talk about this: the doctor just sighs, and says sometimes yes, sometimes no. The famous sensuality of Brando's mouth, brow and eyes roars with the question, but the brave film stays hushed because of censorship. There is no talk, and no attempt at awkward sexual congress.

To research the film, Brando enters a military hospital in Van Nuys that is mentioned in the prologue to the film. Call this Method, or good sense; he wants to see how these broken bodies do move, as well as how they talk, joke and feel. It is said that he spends the three-week rehearsal period in Van Nuys, pretending to be paralyzed. You can feel that education in the detail of a film that employs many handicapped veterans as supporting players.

One can imagine the range of experience that Brando absorbs there. He becomes part of the wounded gang. One night a group of the wheelchair guys goes out to a bowling alley. They are then approached by a devout and well-meaning old lady who tells them how much she admires them, and how they must continue to believe in God with all their might—and then, who knows, they may walk again. Brando's dark humor plays upon the old lady. He says is that so? What do I have to do? And she says he must pray. So Brando becomes a clenched figure of prayer and then he begins to rise from his wheelchair—he stands, he staggers, he moves, he's walking—he's dancing. And the veterans think this is the funniest thing they've ever seen.

That's too much for *The Men*: it cannot find a place for that kind of humor, any more than it can show tumbling paraplegic sex. In the same way, it has to stomach Teresa Wright as the sweetheart. Wright can be a very good actress: a few years earlier she was superb in Alfred Hitchcock's *Shadow of a Doubt*. She is an established star, whose presence helps the picture get made. She has been in *Mrs. Miniver*, *The Little Foxes* and *The Best Years of Our Lives*, in which she is the reliable sweetheart who saves Dana Andrews from despair when he comes home from the war.

She is also entirely wrong chemistry for Marlon Brando. Wright's husband, screenwriter Niven Busch, warns her of this, tells her it's going

Point Guard

Making *The Men*, Brando lived with paraplegics in a veterans' hospital. Under this handicap, he seemed more than ever one of the great physical actors.

Bottom's Up

"I just cut my throat" by agreeing to star opposite Brando in *The Men*, said Teresa Wright later. Her miscasting hampered an already compromised film.

to be the guy's film. But she is ardent; she wants to do it. And somehow no one notices that she has one kind of happiness in her bright eyes and old-fashioned face, while he has far darker dreams in his hooded, sullen, hurt eyes. Brando is so overwhelmingly sensual, you cannot believe how—before the war—he ever fell for this girl.

There is another film begging to be made in *The Men*. It would use Brando's thwarted, antisocial energy so that he rebuffs his sweet girl, and finds . . . well, what in 1949 would have been called a slut, or worse. A hooker perhaps—a rough woman, not pretty or demure, not filled with hope or illusion, but the kind of woman who knows enough to offer Ken rare sexual relief. Of course, Hollywood could not make that film then. Maybe it still wouldn't do it. But it's very telling that Brando's presence and his terrific energy as an actor make one search for the question or the possibility.

That very tough, grown-up film might even build Ken's contempt for the hypocritical society along with his own blunt awareness of his new physical limits. There's a moment in the hospital where he uses his crutches to smash up a room. That scene has a power still, a release that could start you thinking of a few of the paraplegics becoming a hold-up gang—something far from the decently accommodated figures *The Men* is grooming. So it's not an honest film, and no amount of daring can conceal that. It's a very unusual film, but straightaway Brando is so good in it as to expose its helpless distance from real shattered lives. Yet in Brando's yearning there is always that sense of "Let me be real."

Still, it is a debut, it is $40,000, it is a first chance to feel the difficulty and the indignity of doing big emotional moments out of order and surrounded by watchful technicians. Brando likes none of those things. Again, he alarms director Fred Zinnemann by seeming out of touch in rehearsal, or until the moment he has to deliver. And once he's delivered, that's it. The film gets good reviews and a lot of respectful attention. No one seems to notice that Marlon Brando is already ten pounds too sleek for a hospitalized veteran in 1949. In truth, he doesn't look exactly right. But he has begun, and he has identified the devout old lady in Americana, that figure he has it in his power to shock.

DESIRE UNDER THE PALMS

A movie of *Streetcar* is bound to be made. In Hollywood, the reputation of the title and its haunting obscurity are too much to be left alone. But the sensational impact felt on stage is not the kind of thing the movies can handle. And so, to this day, the celebrated movie—the one Brando says he prefers to the play, and which sometimes the volatile Williams endorsed—has a prim, tidy ending where Stella whispers to her new baby that they're never going back to that Stanley again. And so, his cries of "Stella!" go unrewarded as the credits come up. And Blanche's flagrant promiscuity and the rape— those are things left for the dirty-minded to pick up on. Of course, that kind of censorship does tend to breed dirty minds in all of us.

The problem threatens from the outset, and along the way it leads to odd ploys. The producer, Irene Selznick, very eager to sell the rights, even entertains the thought of having Lillian Hellman (at $5,000 a week) write a version with a happier ending. Both Elia Kazan and Marlon Brando will say, later on, that they are reluctantly brought to the party. Brando does not mention the gelding of the play, but Kazan will proclaim how he was deceived and betrayed by those at Warner Brothers and the Catholic Legion of Decency. Kazan will write a letter to the *New York Times* about it, full of artistic integrity and indignation, enough perhaps for letting himself off the hook for having signed on and directed the film that can never quite be the play in 1950. In other words, you have to be foolish, ambitious or self-deceiving to disregard the likely obstacles.

Brando's approach is fascinating, and instructive. Whatever his reluctance, or his feeling of the play and Stanley being part of his history, he pushes the opening offer of $50,000 from Warner Brothers up to $80,000. "I've heard it said that I sold out to Hollywood," he says. "In a way it's true, but I knew exactly what I was doing." To hear his explanation, the young actor is profoundly cynical on the eve of his second picture, and his mercenary approach is offset only by how calculated he is. For already he has come to the conclusion that "Hollywood stands for avarice, phoniness, greed, crassness and bad taste, but when you act in a movie,

Not Quite the Play
The poster hinted at racy scenes, but the film version of *Streetcar* was considerably tamer than the Broadway play—a problem for many films of Tennessee Williams's works.

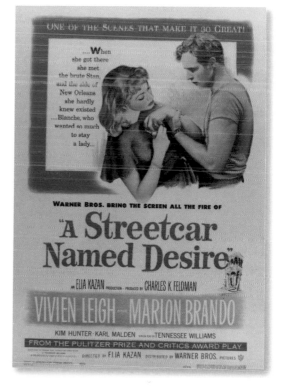

you only have to work three months a year, then you can do as you please for the rest."

There's something refreshing in that country-boy candor, maybe. It is so much cleaner than the elaborate way in which Elia Kazan always depicts himself as the victim of compromise, intrigue, impossible dilemma and treachery—instead of just the chronic follower of his own nose. But there's something crushing in the young actor's being so alienated so early, and something tragic in how helpless he is with his own vast indolence. Fifty years ago, we can see the outline of what is to come, and feel his own smug helplessness.

Of course, the film of *Streetcar* is better than that sounds. In the end, Kazan resolves to keep as close as possible to the text. He also abandons early plans to open the play up, to bring Blanche's past to life. Instead, Kazan agrees with history that he has made a masterpiece on stage and that he will do his best to record it for posterity.

There is one quibble from Warner Brothers. They want a movie star name in the picture. Brando is not that yet, because the arrangements are made before *The Men* has been released. But Jessica Tandy is the sacrificial victim. Kazan and the others are contrite and guilty about this, but the half-cunning, half-forgiving Kazan does allow that maybe he wants some fresh excitement, a new person to work with. Selznick wonders about Olivia de Havilland (who has recently won an Oscar for *To Each His Own*, as well as nominations for *The Snake Pit* and *The Heiress*). There is even a thought that De Havilland and her sister, Joan Fontaine, might play the DuBois sisters. Other names in consideration are Jane Wyman and Jennifer Jones. But the decision comes down in favor of Vivien Leigh, who has played Blanche in the London production of *Streetcar* —with Bonar Colleano as her Stanley and with her husband, Laurence Olivier, as director. Selznick sees that production; she sees how wrong-headed Olivier is on the play and she observes the pitiful state of Leigh—physically ill and very close to a mental breakdown. Both ailments are exacerbated by playing Blanche. But Irene thinks Leigh will serve the film well as a star presence. After all, it was David Selznick who had had a hunch about Leigh for *Gone With the Wind* and Scarlett O'Hara— her first southern belle.

It says something for Leigh that, even in her own distress, she joins a very seasoned cast and dominates the movie. The silliness in Blanche—or that potential— dissolves and is replaced by an authentic tragic grandeur. This does not come easily or quickly. Vivien Leigh is very accustomed to being an outward emblem of English good manners. She addresses her fellows formally, and Brando thinks this is a riot of affectation. But she perseveres, and plainly sees the talent in Brando. She learns to tease him

Vivien's Way
On the London stage, Vivien Leigh played Blanche like a prostitute— and even consulted with real ladies of the night for pointers. She got so caught up in the plot that she suffered a serious mental breakdown.

a little, and to respond well to his earthy humor. He is intimidated by her perfume. She says that she likes to smell sweet. Doesn't he? And he tells her he'd rather shower in a gob of spit. But they get on, gradually. She enjoys his wicked imitations of Laurence Olivier doing Shakespeare. He cannot fail to see her courage and her instinctive feeling for Blanche.

Kazan has early difficulties with Leigh. He has to train her out of the bad habits Olivier's production have set up. But, little by little, Kazan notes with his normal satisfaction, everything works out to his way of thinking. And just as Leigh becomes commanding in the film, so Stanley recedes and takes up his proper position as a supporting actor. The movie is about Blanche in a way that Kazan never managed to achieve onstage with Jessica Tandy. To that extent, the film exists now somewhere between a record of 1947 and the definitive version of the play.

That difference helps explain a point of controversy. *Streetcar* the movie gets twelve Academy Award nominations. It wins for Leigh, Karl Malden, Kim Hunter and for the sets. It loses for Kazan, for Screenplay (credited to Tennessee Williams), for Picture and for Brando, who is beaten by Humphrey Bogart in *The African Queen*.

There is some argument over this, for Brando already has the emotional support of a young group in show business, just as he seems to represent a new generation of actors. But Brando has done and said nothing to make himself agreeable, let alone popular, with the Academy voters. And, as he says himself, Humphrey Bogart has been doing his thing for decades and has come along with a rare character study—acting rather than mere being—in *The African Queen*. Give the old-timer his chance. Brando says he doesn't give a damn about the Oscars. And the Oscars easily adopt a similar indifference to him.

Already, it has become Marlon Brando's psychic need to hold a position of moral superiority. In terms of his struggle with Hollywood, that is all very well: he and the town can look after themselves. But later on, Brando has ugly things to say about Vivien Leigh: "Like Blanche, she slept with almost everybody and was beginning to dissolve mentally and to fray at the ends physically. I might have given her a tumble if it hadn't been for Larry Olivier. I'm sure he knew she was playing around, but like a lot of husbands I've known, he pretended not to see it, and I liked him too much to invade his chicken coop."

High Water Mark
During filming of *Streetcar*, Humphrey Bogart (here in a scene from *African Queen*) stopped by the set to get a glimpse of Brando, the new kid on the block. Little did he know he'd be competing against the kid for an Oscar.

JOHN STEINBECK'S
VIVA ZAPATA!

20th CENTURY-FOX

MARLON BRANDO · JEAN PETERS
PRODUCED BY DARRYL F. ZANUCK · DIRECTED BY ELIA KAZAN · WRITTEN BY JOHN STEINBECK
with ANTHONY QUINN · JOSEPH WISEMAN · ARNOLD MOSS · ALAN REED · MARGO · HAROLD GORDON · LOU GILBERT · MILDRED DUNNOCK

Mexican Romance
The poster for *Viva Zapata!* (above) stressed the film's adventure and romance—and played down the populist social agenda. Brando found plenty of romance himself on the set.

Gunslinger
To prepare for his first costume role, Brando (right) lived among peasants in Mexico, and boned up on Spanish. Some realism didn't work: For a scene in which he was to be drunk, he insisted on actually getting drunk. It had to be scrapped.

So, not yet thirty, Brando's attitude to acting is to do movies for the money, the long vacation and the easy opportunity to sleep around. It's odd how close that coarseness comes to the personality of Stanley Kowalski. It's well known that the distraught Leigh was deeply affected and injured by being Blanche, but maybe Brando was made less sensitive by his years as Stanley and the adulation that followed.

He has a relationship going with Roberta Haynes, his agent's onetime girlfriend; he is often seen with Shelley Winters, a New York acquaintance, who is now in Los Angeles; and there is already some talk that he may be in the process of acquiring, or borrowing, another blonde from Elia Kazan—Marilyn Monroe. In his continuing observation of Brando, Kazan notes that there will be a stream of women, none committed to, none of them meaning as much as the gang of men friends Brando keeps in tow. The women are like the acting: proof of an extraordinary talent or appetite that cannot yet discover a real interest in the exercise.

BORDER TOWNS

In Kazan's mind, at least, there was another reason why he had been overlooked in the Academy awards for *Streetcar*: the pressure on him from the House Un-American Activities Committee to name names from his quite brief Communist past (1933-5) was building. There was more talk in Hollywood that he might be "unsound," and thus unemployable. The terrible argument had begun in his own mind as to whether he owed it to his career (and the fate of his nation) to give testimony. *Viva Zapata!* needs to be seen and felt in the atmosphere of that torment.

The idea for a film about Emiliano Zapata had existed for several years in talks between Kazan and the novelist John Steinbeck. Indeed, the novelist had been laboring over a script, trying to carve an acceptably Hollywood story out of Zapata's career. Coming from Morelos in southern Mexico, Zapata—an Indian of very little education—had adopted the cause of land ownership and agrarian reform. He had opposed successive Mexican governments and become a hero to the impoverished. But he was always reluctant to be leader of his country or to get involved in politics. The real man was undoubtedly savage in his tactics, and there are legends of his chronic womanizing.

The project ends up at Twentieth Century-Fox, where studio head Darryl Zanuck is inclined to cast Tyrone Power (or even Anthony Quinn) as Zapata. The swashbuckling Power seems appropriate: in the script, Zapata marries his sweetheart (played by Jean Peters), is portrayed as stoic, noble and simple, and is deeply attached to a white stallion, which becomes the final image of his undying appeal.

On the other hand, this is a script that addresses the need for peasant ownership of the land; that looks squarely at the hopeless corruption of so many would-be reform governments in Mexico; and which has at its most sinister figure, the commissar-like Fernando (Joseph Wiseman), a classically heartless and cynical party official who is out to manipulate the naïve Zapata—and who very well embodies Elia Kazan's sense of the odious Communist Party organizers who had once ordered him around.

There is a very telling situation in the film: at the outset, as Zapata is part of a delegation sent to appeal to the Mexican president, he is picked out as a troublemaker, and his name is circled on a list of names. Then later, when Zapata himself has come to power, he finds himself doing the same thing with the name of another rebellious peasant (played by Henry Silva). It is a very good movie moment, and it surely reveals a director agonizing over the naming of names himself. Which doesn't mean that Kazan bothered to explain the subtext of the moment to Brando.

Kazan is determined that Brando shall be Zapata: he has the sense to realize how earlier "Mexican" films from Hollywood have been a travesty of that nation. He mounts a screen test, with Brando and Julie Harris, and though Zanuck is as appalled as others that he can't hear what Brando is saying for mumbling, still he sees and feels a new reality in the actor. For Brando is going to do all he can to look like a Mexican Indian. There is a second test (with Peters) in which Brando begins to acquire his Mexican look—slanted, narrow eyes; a drooping mustache; full black hair; deep tan; and a kind of Aztec cast to his features. Zanuck accepts the casting and is then persuaded to put up $100,000 for Brando—the same sum as that paid Kazan, who has been bargained down to that level because of fears that his political scandal may erupt.

Originally, it had been Kazan's hope to film in Mexico itself. But the several ministries and departments there involved in the project demand

BOMBS AWAY

May 1951
• The United States tests the first hydrogen bomb at the Pacific atoll of Eniwetok. The bomb, which harnesses the elemental power of the sun, is hundreds of times more powerful than the first atom bombs.

Hamming it Up
While shooting *Viva Zapata!*, Brando began to empathize with the Mexican leader, who was torn between helping the poor and getting ahead.

script approval, and so eventually the director settles for small towns on the Texas side of the border—notably Del Rio and Roma. It is there in the summer of 1951, in heat well over 100 degrees, that the cast and the crew go to film. You can still feel the glaring heat in the film's imagery, and there is a thoroughly sweaty air to the proceedings that is unusual for that period and suitably deromanticized.

Brando plunges into the research involved. He goes to live in small Mexican villages for weeks before the shooting. He revels in his elaborate make-up. And he declares that Mexico is a paradise—a slow, sleepy, journalist-free world. He plays with the animals and the children. He goes swimming with Kazan in the evenings in the Rio Grande. And he develops an elaborate flirtatious relationship with Peters—no matter that she is being courted by Howard Hughes. Whether or not Peters yields to Brando is lost in the legend of old Mexico. But it is clear that they have a lot of fun, and to judge by her naughty smile in the film itself we may conclude that no time was wasted. Not that Brando is ever single-minded in these matters: he surveys the Mexican women and discovers a very appealing older woman, Movita Castenada, who has a film history. She was actually in *Mutiny on the Bounty* with Clark Gable in 1935, when they had an affair. Movita is humorous, beautiful, unusually wise and sympathetic, and a special relationship develops.

With his customary astuteness, Kazan has cast Anthony Quinn as Zapata's brother—not just because Quinn was considered for the lead, but because Quinn is Brando's biggest rival as Stanley Kowalski. To spice that stew more, Kazan whispers to both actors that the other is hostile, suspicious and difficult. So a standoff ensues—all good for the warring relationship between the brothers in the story, and the more likely to make the flamboyant Quinn show off. Thus, his brother is as flashy and extroverted as Brando's Zapata is taciturn, dignified and inarticulate. In time, the two actors discover the simple trick that has been played on them, but they don't really get close, and literally engage in pissing contests. (The longer carry wins.)

The unit returns to Los Angeles for interiors, and it is then that Kazan fights his forlorn battles to defend *Streetcar* from censorship. And in the same season, actually while waiting for the Oscars to be announced for 1951, on January 14, 1952, Kazan goes to Washington, D.C., and names

ARMS AND THE MAN

In the summer of 1953, on an impulse, Brando decided that he would mount a summer-season play with a few hard up friends. He would take a modest salary himself, so that the others could earn some real money. Was it a joke? No, not quite. He elects to do George Bernard Shaw's *Arms and the Man* with himself (Sergius) and William Redfield (Bluntschli) in the lead roles. The production actually happens, in July 1953, at a summer-

In plays like *Arms and the Man,* first produced in 1894, George Bernard Shaw (above) satirized romantic ideas of love and war.

stock theatre in Matunuck, Rhode Island, and then moves on to three other New England towns. But Brando forgets that Sergius has one long speech, never learns it, and when the speech comes up says whatever comes into his head. The *Boston Post* said Brando "made a fool of himself." It was the last time he appeared on stage.

names to the committee. In March 1952, just after the night *Streetcar* wins so many Oscars, *Viva Zapata!* opens.

Zapata wins mixed reviews. Why not? It is a very uneasy mix of radical history and the same old sentimental dismissal of Mexico as a hopeless place. But Brando gets a very good reception. Hedda Hopper, who has had a hard time getting him to give her a decent or polite interview, admits that he has done a superb job as the Mexican leader. A year later, as Oscar season comes around, both Quinn and Brando are nominated. Quinn wins the Supporting Actor Oscar, but Brando loses to Gary Cooper for *High Noon* (the Western made by the production trio from *The Men*—Stanley Kramer, Fred Zinnemann and Carl Foreman).

By then, however, the news of Kazan's testimony is widespread. Brando seems to have learned of it at different times and in different degrees of detail, candor or attention. The actor's first instinct may be to ignore the matter and

The Togs of War

Marlon was totally relaxed on the *Caesar* set (right), even though his personal life was in turmoil— tension with his live-in girlfriend Movita Castenada, liaisons with Rita Moreno and Katy Jurado, and flirting with costars Greer Garson and Deborah Kerr.

Nothing to Fear

Brando (above, with James Mason in *Julius Caesar*) "could move into unknown territory without spooking himself," said director Joseph Mankiewicz, "relaxed, unburdened by the awareness of anything except his inner promptings."

trust a friend. But Kazan has offended his generation. Indeed, he will never be forgiven by many old associates. It is a situation or a test that Brando cannot avoid. And he is heard to condemn his great director and to promise that he will never work with him again.

So be it. Brando at that time is widely reckoned as someone more interested in women, or his pet raccoon, Russell, than in pretending to be betrayed by political actions. But he is very close to Kazan and he is a very sharp observer of human behavior. He enjoys a nearly magical rapport with Kazan; he trusts and respects the director, and has the capacity always to absorb direction and then come up with something Kazan could never imagine in advance.

In other words, their working closeness is too great for Brando to claim complete unawareness of what is happening. He is at a point—one pioneered by Kazan—where he will have to make the attempt to distinguish between acting for its own sake and living out larger issues as if they are as real as the heat in Roma, Texas, and the look on Jean Peters' face. An actor ignores content, or ideas, by burying his head in the sand, or by being interested only in himself. One way or another, Marlon Brando is being dragged away from mere acting and forced into the public world of issues and controversy. He will play that new role, but maybe it is never his favorite.

TO PRAISE CAESAR

A crisis is coming for Brando. One can feel it in the mounting struggle between actor and celebrity, between the urge to mine the anonymous force of brutish humanity and that appalling public exposure—of being known and named in advance, the fatal ruin for any actor who longs to protect his own nothingness as the soil in which becoming begins.

But the tension is there, too, in the way this young Nebraska lout refuses to grow up, refuses to come of age, to mature, to settle—for those dread ends seem only to defy his adolescent faith in what it is to be an actor. He would call it being ready and able to change forever, but that is only another way of saying: Do not grow up. It is there in the hapless failure of his ties to his parents and his chronic, untied links to so many other women.

But if you want the flat-out, unequivocal statement of the urge to move off violently in opposite directions, it's there in the way he does *Julius Caesar* and *The Wild One* in the space of a few months—as if only in showing how he can do anything or everything he lives up to the absurd strain of being "Marlon Brando." Years later, it will be recognized that in his first six movies,

from *The Men* to *On the Waterfront*, he was astonishing, soaring, climbing. Then nothing was ever the same again. Don't minimize or exclude from this the agony for such a kid of becoming thirty.

From the outset, *Julius Caesar* is meant to be one of Metro-Goldwyn-Mayer's prestigious productions. Its producer is John Houseman, once partner to Orson Welles in the Mercury Theatre—indeed, in 1938 they produce a modern-dress version of the play, renamed simply *Caesar*, with Welles himself as Brutus, intended as an allusion to the Europe of Hitler and Mussolini. Houseman's movie project has no such stress in 1952: it is culture for the masses, done with as much showmanship as possible.

Houseman assembles his cast carefully. John Gielgud is a natural Cassius; Louis Calhern has the authority for Caesar; and James Mason will be the troubled Brutus. Gielgud proposes his English colleague, Paul Scofield, for Marc Antony. Houseman reflects, and may feel the gap between Scofield's essentially quiet tone and the rabble-rousing rhetoric of Antony's funeral speech. He has a brain wave: what about Marlon Brando? He recalls the searing speech Brando made in the Ben Hecht play, *A Flag Is Born*. MGM is fascinated by the idea of a hot young star in Shakespeare, but everyone doubts whether the notorious mumbler can actually speak the verse.

Though later Brando will say it was "asinine" of him to try the role, he is immediately interested. He even makes a tape of several key speeches for Houseman and his director, Joseph L. Mankiewicz, to be submitted as a test. Played to those unaware, there is widespread guessing—is it Olivier, Jose Ferrer or some other trained Shakespearean? Houseman is persuaded. When Dore Schary, production chief at MGM, hears the tape, he agrees to the casting and is not deterred by press incredulity.

It is Brando's concession that he will try Antony for a mere $40,000 (twice Gielgud's fee, but a significant pay cut for the American).

Mankiewicz and Brando use a small addition to his nose to make him seem more Roman, but as soon as his hair is cut and combed forward there is an appreciable antique cast to his look. He trains for the early scene in which Antony is half-naked for the rite where he must run through the city touching virgins to endure their fertility. And Brando will duly flirt with the film's ladies, Greer Garson and Deborah Kerr. Yet everyone on the picture is impressed by the seriousness of his approach.

The Stud Meets the Bard
Brando as Marc Antony in *Julius Caesar*, a picture that brought Shakespeare to the masses and made Roman haircuts big news.

He has coaching and advice with the verse. He has John Gielgud as a teacher, as Gielgud becomes increasingly convinced of Brando's ability. Still, the great funeral speech is an enormous challenge for an actor who has had no experience with Shakespeare or with such large, formal scenes. He goes back to Stella Adler in preparing the scene, and he charms Houseman with their startled discovery—that in Shakespeare there is no subtext; everything is there in the words; all the actor has to do is to let them flow through his voice, his presence and his being. It's a moment at which modern naturalism finds itself able to shake hands with the classical tradition.

Mankiewicz films the Forum speech as best he can with Antony and the crowd together, as well as many cutaway reaction close-ups. This scheme involves over a week of work in which Brando has to do the speech over and over again. It strains his voice, but Houseman for one is delighted at the young actor's commitment:

"The real credit goes to Brando himself, who during that long week of shooting— many times each day, in close-up and long shot, in whole or in part, and even when the cameras were all aimed at the crowd and not on him—went through the speech, over and over, without once losing his energy or his concentration. When he faltered or flubbed a line he would stop, apologize, compose himself and start afresh.

"He never pleaded fatigue or questioned the necessity for so much seemingly repetitious coverage. When the scene came to be edited, his performance benefited greatly from the number and variety of 'takes' we had of each phase of that long, demanding speech."

The proof is in a film that, fifty years later, is still the definitive version of *Julius Caesar* offered to students of the play. Moreover, he deserves to have his own dedication underlined when, sadly, there will be so many contrary reports later. He was proving himself; he had people like Gielgud, Mankiewicz and Houseman to impress. But he is remarkable in the film— fierce, subtle, handsome, a hurt son as well as an emerging manipulator. This Antony is not the hardest role ever written—not nearly as challenging as the Antony who meets Cleopatra. Still, *Julius Caesar* is the film that carries Brando from cult figure and brilliant rogue to authentic actor in the eyes of a universal audience. The gravest doubts fall away: here is a man who might do

Critical Mass

Shakespeare's name is above the title, but Brando looms largest in this poster for *Julius Caesar*. The film won rave reviews, especially for Brando.

HELL ON WHEELS

Hell's Angels patriarch Sonny Barger (center) poses with a few of his followers.

The Hell's Angels motorcycle gang and its various imitators owed their existence to an early form of mobile hippie culture, the Harley-Davidson motorcycle, and small-town paranoia. Over the July 4th weekend of 1947, a gathering of machines and riders in Hollister, California—a small town in agricultural country, just east of Monterey and Salinas—prompted panic tales of take-over and unrestrained outlawry. It became the basis for

The Wild One. Not that the real Hell's Angels weren't dangerous. The 1967 book *Hell's Angels* by Hunter Thompson makes clear the degree to which the bikers, led by Sonny Barger, ran on liquor, drugs, testosterone and violence. And the gangs can still be seen in glowing convoys on western highways, even if some of the "boys" claim their pension now.

anything. (He is nominated for Best Actor again, the third year in a row, and loses to William Holden's seasoned persona in *Stalag 17*.)

Gielgud is so impressed and moved that he invites Brando to go back to London with him, to join him and Scofield in a season of classic theater. He offers to direct Brando as Hamlet. As it happens, Marlon smiles and says thank you, no—he really wants to go scuba diving.

For every skeptic who says Brando cannot carry Shakespeare, there is a supporter who wishes he would not be Johnny, the biker-boy in *The Wild One*. At a length of seventy-nine minutes, this always looks like early Roger Corman, an exploitation B picture, more than social commentary. Yet that seems to be its original intent, based on incidents involving early manifestations of the Hell's Angels.

It is another Stanley Kramer production, written by John Paxton and directed by Laslo Benedek, in which a bunch of Hollywood actors, most of them too old for it, masquerade as juvenile delinquents. It is a kind of *Rebel Without a Cause* done without the conviction or the urban atmosphere of that film. Brando leaps at the part: beyond playing with his raccoon, he would rather act with a motorbike than with anyone else. He likes the leather jacket, the cap, and it is a shining example of his naïveté that he cannot see that he is a degree or two too plump, and at twenty-nine verging on the ridiculous. Even as it opens, *The Wild One* has too many moments that are not just ridiculous but camp. Not least of these is the famous repartee—"What are you rebelling against, Johnny?" and the answer, half-sighing, half-snarling, "Whaddya got?" This is too glib, too insolent to match the real, tumescent unruliness of American teenagers. *The Wild One* is forever a lurid part of Brando's image and legend. But it is his first wretched picture, and it goes to his tender heart:

"More than most parts I've played . . . I related to Johnny. . . . Like Johnny, I have always resented authority. I have been constantly discomfited by people telling me what to do, and have always thought that Johnny took refuge in his lifestyle because he was wounded. . . . He had been so disappointed in life that it was difficult for him to express love, but beneath his hostility lay a desperate yearning and desire to feel love because he'd had so little of it. I could have just as easily been describing myself."

Sensitive Rebel
As leader of the Black Rebels in *The Wild One*, Brando casts his gaze (somewhere) on Mary Murphy. Their dialog now seems hokey, but much of it was watered down by censors, who feared the film would inspire juvenile delinquency or, worse, communism.

EARLY WOMEN

So disappointed, yet so successful. Is this real dysfunction, or is it the available scenario for a young patient determined to be interesting for his psychotherapist? Brando has difficulties with his parents, to be sure; neither of them is the easiest person in the world. He says he has had so little love. But the mother has moved to New York, to be near him and his success in a field that once was hers. And the gruff father is still a man to whom Marlon entrusts most of his money for investing. Things could be worse.

As he rehearses for the stage production of *Streetcar*, he lives with Wally Cox in a cold-water flat. Wally and Marlon and Wally's girlfriend invite Shelley Winters to dinner: canned tomato soup; cold cauliflower dipped in sour cream; fried grapefruit with brown sugar. It's cold in the flat, and so Marlon later invites her into his bed. "My body generates a great deal of heat," he promises her. And she admits he was right.

There is an affair, driven by Winters' adulation of him as an actor. When she eventually sees him in *Streetcar*, she goes backstage to congratulate him. He's in the shower, and she has time to see a Charles Atlas instruction book, and maybe a hundred slips of papers with girls' names and phone numbers. Then there is the collection of hotel room keys. She asks what they're for and Brando grins. So many women—famous women from show business and café society —have come backstage already and left their room key. He's working his way through them, he says, as research. Winters decides that it's probably time to end her physical relationship with Marlon

Not that Shelley Winters is unduly prudish or cautious, or concentrating on getting married and settling down. But she has seen the side of life that seems to many other observers—and which he frequently and proudly proclaims—as his reason for being. Sleeping with women. Well, why not? He is young, healthy and phenomenally attractive; he has burst upon the world in a production that asserts his sex appeal; he has become a celebrity and an actor, so that it is half taken for granted by most women that such a force of life must move on. The inquiry in sex is, quite simply, the intimate knowledge of other people: and Brando is the kind of actor who loves to enter into a kind of osmotic process with strangers, absorbing them, filling up his own empty places.

There is no way to know or list all the names: when the journalist Joe Hyams attempts this, he concludes that "it takes a statistician rather than a reporter." Moreover, many of the women seem

That's Entertainment
Firebrand Puerto Rican
entertainer Rita Moreno, who
slipped in and out of Brando's
orbit over the years, is the only
woman to have won an Oscar
(*West Side Story*), an Emmy
(actually two, for *The Muppet
Show* and *The Rockford Files*), a
Grammy (music from *The Electric
Company*) and a Tony (*The Ritz*).

reconciled to his infidelity. They may not even see it as something worthy of blame, or guilt. He is less fickle than motile—the way of sperm, after all. He is entirely candid about the extent of his sexual appetite, and about his reluctance to settle. We do not have to agree that he is exceptional at sex; instead, he is unusual in that he pursues sex for its own sake, and is not often drawn into claims of love and eternity—the rhetoric that impedes so many of us. So lovers accept that they will be dropped, and then reclaimed, depending on where he is, his mood, the chance of meeting. Never in love, he is never out of love. Liking sex with this woman, and that one, he is ready to repeat the experience. So in many cases women become fixtures in his life, only briefly in high fashion but never forgotten.

Well, you can hear some women say, isn't that a pretty theory—for it is promiscuity dressed up as philosophy. So there are women who reject Brando and who despise his slippery, selfish ways. And he lets those ones go. He is not, apparently, too much interested in conversation—let alone argument—with his women.

Movita, the actress encountered in Mexico during *Viva Zapata!*, comes back to Los Angeles with him. Movita is a good deal older than Brando: she is likely thirty-five. And she has been married to a boxer named Jack Doyle. Still is, it turns out, but that doesn't deter her early urge to be Mrs. Brando. She knows a good deal more about life than he knows, and she beats him regularly at chess. At first she tries to set up a home for them, but Brando shies away from such tenderness. Arguments build. The love affair cools. But Movita is seldom out of the picture. One old girlfriend, Roberta Haynes, observes Movita urging Brando to be less of a slob—pick up your clothes, get them cleaned, grow up. In a way, Movita becomes something of a mother, and she specializes in wise sayings about the unruly boy.

There are affairs with other Latin actresses—Katy Jurado and Rita Moreno—and there are so many other casual pickups, so many of them Latinas or women of color. The pattern is the same: sexual infatuation on both sides, often a shared living arrangement, and then difficulty, moroseness and alienation from Brando if he is nagged, lectured or criticized. But there are times when he comes close to marriage.

Early in 1954 (his time of crisis), just as he is about to film *Desirée*, he meets a small, dark French girl at a party given by Stella Adler. Her name is Josanne Mariani-Berenger, and she is nineteen. They live together briefly, then Brando orders her out of his house. Other women intervene. Josanne goes back to France, to her home in Bandol. But then Brando pursues her and a French newspaper has her father announcing the engagement. In America, Rita Moreno tells the press, "I was amazed . . . But he seemed to be a lost soul. Looking for a niche."

By November even Brando admits that he intends to marry Josanne. She returns to America and there are fights in public. On one occasion, she accuses Marlon and Christian Marquand of being lovers. Josanne finds a roommate, a starlet named Ursula Andress, and Andress manages to have Brando for herself in a few days. And then Brando is outraged to discover that Josanne has posed nude for a series of paintings! It all ends short of marriage.

And another woman who has been in and out of Brando's bed during 1954 is Marilyn Monroe. When did they meet? On the set of *Viva Zapata!* in Texas. For at that time, Monroe is having an affair with Elia Kazan. She comes to visit, but then Kazan's wife decides on a Mexican holiday. Once she arrives, Brando becomes Marilyn's companion. It may not mean too much at the time for Brando and Monroe, but Kazan has been for several years now the dominant male figure in Brando's life. And Kazan is one of those men, consummate betrayers, who always feels that he has been victimized by others. The crisis develops.

The actor is deeply troubled over his relationship with the precious director—and

His Fiancée?

When French starlet Josanne Mariani-Berenger landed at New York's Idlewild Airport in 1954, she cuddled a photo of Brando and denied that her engagement to the star was a publicity stunt.

Kazan may be the best analyst Brando will ever know. He would be a lot to lose. But on the set of *Julius Caesar*, he is heard lamenting his own predicament—whether to condemn Kazan, or to stay loyal to the man. Joseph Mankiewicz, director of *Julius Caesar*, finds Brando in tears one day. He asks what's the matter and it all tumbles out about Kazan. "What'll I do when I see him?" Brando asks. As Mankiewicz sees it, there is nothing less than worship for Kazan on Brando's part.

Over the next few months, as Kazan suffers the backlash from informing, Brando talks more than anyone that undecided should. He sounds foolish, pontificating that really, no one with integrity should work for a man like Kazan, but then allowing as how maybe he would—once or twice, at least—if only because Kazan was so good for him. All the women may be a diversion from this tougher pain, especially if one grants the truth in the observation that, despite all the women in his life, Marlon Brando is more dependent on ties to men. And he remembers that that insight comes from Kazan himself.

LIFE AND ART

Nor should we miss the crisis that was overtaking Kazan, or his zeal for it. "Gadg" Kazan (the early nickname, short for Gadget, stuck for life although he professed to despise it) was born Elia Kazanjoglou, in 1909, in the suburbs of Constantinople. He comes to New York at the age of four, the son of a rug

dealer. And the family does well, but never well enough to hide Kazan's feeling that he is one of the great ugly men of his time, a force of nature and ambition propelled by his own disadvantages. He is a man who can hardly avoid watching Marlon Brando and saying to himself, look at that absurdly beautiful, lazy, foolish guy. If only…

Kazan attends Williams College and nurses a portrait of himself as the swarthy alien in a smug WASP club, ignored by the beautiful blond women, patronized by the guys with names like Chip, Bud and Brad. Time will tell that Elia has the lust and the sexual drive to take all their women, and the genius to be outstanding in film and theatre. He joins the Group Theatre in the 1930s. He is himself an actor before he realizes that direction is more suited to his desire for control. In the years right after the war, he rises very rapidly: he directs *All My Sons*, *Streetcar* and *Death of a Salesman* on

Marilyn and Arthur
After Elia Kazan revealed the names of communists to HUAC, his friendship with playwright Arthur Miller was shattered. Pointedly, Miller then married Kazan's mistress, Marilyn Monroe (seen here with Miller in 1960) and never named names, despite tremendous pressure.

the stage; and in Hollywood he begins to make movies with *A Tree Grows in Brooklyn*, *Boomerang!* and *Gentleman's Agreement*. These are proficient yet impersonal pictures: on film, Kazan lacks the acuity and focus he can bring to a scene on stage. But *Gentleman's Agreement* wins the Oscar for Best Picture. And there is no doubting his reputation as a supreme director of actors. In that legend, no event means more than his discovery of Marlon Brando and the way he brings Stanley to dangerous life in *Streetcar*.

But Kazan wants more. He wants to be an artist, and he wants to make movies that are widely accepted as his. On stage, the best director serves the playwright; with film, there is a new idea gaining ground—that the medium might belong to directors. So he needs to find himself in that medium. To do that—I am not suggesting that the whole thing is so cold-blooded or determined—he makes himself his own subject. He testifies to the House Un-American Activities Committee. He names names, but in doing so he becomes an enormous character—a villain, if you like, a chronic careerist who will sell out to stay in work. But an interesting character—as well as that ugly man who somehow gets all the women, even Marilyn Monroe.

We are describing a man with a practical intelligence and ambition that only exposes the sunny immaturity in Marlon Brando. Kazan has had a plan for a year or two to do a movie set against the New York waterfront and its racketeering. With Arthur Miller, then a natural friend, he has developed a script called *The Hook*. But after his testimony, the bond with Miller is severed and the project lapses. Then Kazan hears that the writer Budd Schulberg—

who also testified to the committee—has another waterfront project. Kazan joins with him, and shapes the project to his own desires—it is the story of Terry Malloy, a washed-up ex-fighter, brother to Charley, big in the Mob, and how Terry undergoes a crisis of conscience so that he feels compelled to inform on his brother and the criminal organization. Terry is the first character in a Kazan movie with whom Kazan himself can feel an intense identity.

And Kazan is set on having Frank Sinatra play Terry Malloy.

There is much good sense in this: Sinatra has just startled the world, and won the Supporting Actor Oscar, with his portrayal of Maggio in *From Here to Eternity*; Sinatra is from Hoboken, New Jersey, a part of the very waterfront of this movie—he knows that world; and, though scrawny, Sinatra is in all likelihood a more damaging puncher and a more credible boxer than the easygoing Brando. Who doubts but that Sinatra would have been riveting in the role? Not Frank. He is hungry for the part.

As for Brando, Kazan has been deeply offended by the things he has been saying about hardly wanting to meet Kazan again, let alone work with him. When producer Sam Spiegel asks, what about Marlon, Kazan "bridled and said I didn't want the son of a bitch in the film, he wasn't right for the part anyway, and I was perfectly happy with Frank."

It is so true to Kazan's confessional book, *A Life*, that he says "I ate shit." Protesting loyalty to Sinatra, he still caved in to Spiegel's campaign on behalf of Brando—"it was what I really wanted." Which is a measure of his instinct as well as Spiegel's feeling that Brando then meant more at the box office. Not that there is a reconciliation between the two old friends. No, Brando grumbles about the part and says he is only doing it because his analyst, Bela Mittelmann, advised that he should. It is to be in his contract that at four o' clock every afternoon he can quit the set to see his doctor. Every day.

Then consider this: it may not prove Brando's needs for a doctor, but it shows the very isolated state in which actors can exist. "I finally decided to do the film," Brando will say, "but what I didn't realize then was that

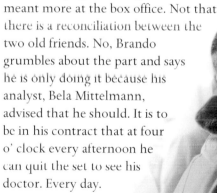

The Vital Link
Did they know it or not? On the set of *On the Waterfront*, director Elia Kazan and Marlon Brando were working together for the last time. They had helped to make each other—that was their bond, and maybe a rivalry too.

Tell It to the Priest

Karl Malden once said that Brando was an inveterate scene-stealer—but he didn't mind, because Brando was so good. "Other people hate him for it, though, because they see it as hogging the act."

On the Waterfront was really a metaphorical argument by Gadg and Budd Schulberg: they made the film to justify finking on their friends. Evidently, as Terry Malloy I represented the spirit of the brave, courageous man who defied evil. Neither Gadg nor Budd Schulberg ever had second thoughts about testifying before that committee."

Here is inadvertent evidence of an actor's inability to read and understand a script—as opposed to checking out what he has to say and do on screen. Marlon Brando understood what *On the Waterfront* was afterward—after he had seen the picture and listened to others talk about it. He could not grasp its nature from the page. Let that settle in: it is not a rare handicap or condition. It is, often, a vital part of the "brilliance" in actors, and a begging reason for us not to revere them.

DOWN TO THE WATER

And so, for $125,000, in cash up front, Brando agrees to do *On the Waterfront*. He sees that as a tough demand on a difficult, low-budget picture: if he will take less money in advance, he is offered ten percent of the profits. That will prove to be a far more substantial sum, but Brando is not subtle with money and he wants to seem like a problem. Sinatra is furious, the more so when he is offered the role of the priest (the Karl Malden part) in recompense. He speaks of Brando as "the most overrated actor in the world."

The picture is shot on the New Jersey waterfront during the winter of 1953–4 in famously harsh conditions. The raw winter light adds a lot to Boris Kaufman's gritty black-and-white photography, but the numbing cold is tough on the cast and crew. And the picture has so little money there is no room for comforts. A further problem, or intimidation, is the presence of onlookers from the Mob itself, uncertain what to make of a big movie that depicts their contribution to American business. Brando observes sarcastically that the Kazan who was so insistent on the removal of Communists is quite willing to make deals with gangsters to get his picture done.

Inwardly, Kazan fumes at all the hardships and at the constant plotting of his producer, Sam Spiegel. But the difficulties only make him fiercer and more determined to succeed. He has become, in his own eyes at least, an outsider again, a pariah. And that is when he is at his best. Moreover, he has a strong story and a cast drawn from the best of the Actors Studio—Eva Marie Saint in the female lead, Karl Malden, Lee J. Cobb and Rod Steiger in the role of Charley Malloy.

On the Waterfront is one of the most celebrated of American pictures, and the one most often cited to describe the power and the legend of Brando. It is also the first film by Kazan in which there exists an unquestioned passion, a burning need to have this story told, a feeling even that the energy and life of the film are embodied in Terry Malloy and the way this has-been is redeeming himself and winning the love of the beautiful girl by informing on his old associates and his own history. It is a telling example of the notion that great damage in real life can be turned into eloquence and power in a work of art.

Once upon a time, On the Waterfront was famous for the shocking cold water of its realism—that feeling that this is what life on the docks was really like. But realism, or naturalism, in film and acting dates quickly. On the Waterfront now looks far more theatrical, far more of the parable that Kazan intended. We have seen too many punch-drunk boxers not to realize that Brando's Terry is a magnificent, romantic creation. Yes, makeup hints at the scars from old cuts, and the famous mumbling style is never better used. But in so many ways, Terry is beautiful and his speeches are not just articulate, but flowery. The intense plea for sympathy in the whole presentation of Terry Malloy now feels like the antithesis of reality. Real, beat-up boxers are beyond being so ingratiating, and they are well past the extraordinary handsomeness of Brando.

There is also a dramatic flaw in the picture. Terry's brother, Charley, is the first lieutenant to Mob boss Johnny Friendly (Lee J. Cobb). He is in many ways the brains of the organization, its least expendable unit. But Schulberg's script works in such a way that as Terry seems likely to inform, so the pressure comes down on Charley to stop him. This is dramatically appealing in that it puts the stress on the fraternal relationship and leads to the scene in the taxicab—one of the most famous scenes in American film—where Charley has to threaten his brother.

ELVIS SINGS

A former movie usher and truck driver named Elvis Presley celebrates his 19th birthday in 1954 by recording his first two songs in a Memphis studio—"Casual Love" and "I'll Never Stand In Your Way." He pays $4 for the privilege.

It's worth noting now that Brando never liked that scene. He is unconvinced that Charley would draw a gun on his brother, and that Terry would then be genuinely afraid. Brothers aren't like that, says Brando. And in practice I think it's highly unlikely that Friendly would use Charley to silence his brother. He would see the very problem that Brando the actor felt. He would leave Charley out of this loop and assign the execution of Terry to other, less involved hands. In the language of *The Godfather* films, Michael (Al Pacino) does not kill Fredo (John Cazale) himself. Brothers do not do such things. merely gives the orders and hears the bump of the faraway shot. That evil, that cynicism, is terrible—monstrous. But a deep truth of family life has been honored.

So on anything like the real waterfront, Charley's dilemma is removed from him. Terry is killed more efficiently. For, as it turns out, not only is the Friendly mob ruined—it has lost its brains, too. Logic and narrative effectiveness might have shaped the story differently. But for Schulberg and Kazan, I think, the conflict of brothers is vital at an emotional level. It is the guts of the parable Kazan pursues; it is the sharpest level of betrayal.

And when they come to film the taxicab scene, that problem, that flaw, remains and obtrudes. Brando says he can't do it the way it's written. Kazan says do it, it will work. They are up against time and money, as always. Carlo Fiore is on the set, watching, and he will say later that as Brando agonizes during rehearsal, Carlo says to him, "The gun-pulling bit hits a bullshit note."

Taxicab Blues
Rod Steiger and Brando in the famous cab-talk scene from *On the Waterfront*. The cab was still; blinds shut out the street—no one cared or noticed.

"What do you mean?" asks Brando.

Carlo explains that the threat and the fear aren't plausible between brothers.

"That's exactly what I've been saying," says Brando.

Who knows what occurs exactly? The chemical interaction in building a scene is so intricate that—just as in life—two people may feel a scene works in different ways. But Kazan nearly accepts this version of their progress. He admits that he didn't really direct the great scene, that Brando and Steiger asked to do an improvisation, and that what we have on screen is how they worked it out together.

Kazan and Brando are far less brothers on this film than in the past. It is to be their last moment together. But Kazan will testify to the remarkable way in which the two actors rescue the scene:

"What was extraordinary about his performance . . . is the contrast of the tough-guy front and the extreme delicacy and gentle cast of his behavior. What other actor, when his brother draws a pistol to force him to do something shameful, would put his hand on the gun and push it away with the gentleness of a caress? Who else could read 'Oh, Charley!' in a tone of reproach that is so loving and so melancholy and suggests that terrific depth of pain? I didn't direct that: Marlon showed me, as he often did, how the scene should be performed."

It's a touching explanation to a great scene—a scene that surmounts some of the film's implausibilities. There's only one sad note. The delays in getting the scene meant that they had no time for the master shot and Brando's close-up before he had to depart for his appointment with Bela Mittelmann. Steiger's close-up remained. It is a courtesy among actors to wait to deliver the feed-lines (off camera) for another actor's close-ups. Brando might have missed one session. But he leaves the set and Kazan has to feed the lines to Rod Steiger. It does not show? Maybe not, but the greatest actors have duties and this was a scene that Brando had helped create.

There is worse, and it is another chain in the crisis. As soon as *On the Waterfront* is cut together, Kazan shows it to Brando. The actor is so depressed by his own performance that he gets up, walks out, and never says a word. In one sense, it hardly matters: the film is a great success. But the crucial bond in Brando's life is broken.

PARADISE LOST

As hard as *On the Waterfront* had been to set up, its success wipes away all clouds. Kazan's uneasy past is erased by the box-office success. When he walks into

A Contender

In this close-up from *On the Waterfront,* we can see how make-up tries to suggest a battered life in the ring, without ever detracting from the actor's beauty.

Add to the few...
the very few...truly
memorable screen
performances:
Marlon Brando as Terry
Malloy in "ON THE
WATERFRONT"...
one of the few...
the very few...
truly great
motion pictures!

COLUMBIA PICTURES presents

MARLON BRANDO

AN ELIA KAZAN PRODUCTION

On The Waterfront

co-starring KARL MALDEN · LEE J. COBB with ROD STEIGER · PAT HENNING and introducing EVA MARIE SAINT
Produced by SAM SPIEGEL   Screen Play by BUDD SCHULBERG   Music by LEONARD BERNSTEIN   Directed by ELIA KAZAN

Watershed Moment

On The Waterfront was the biggest
hit to date of Brando's career—
"full-blown cinema art," said
Bosley Crowther in the *New York
Times*. Overnight, Brando's salary
tripled.

Jack Warner's office and says he wants
to make *East of Eden*, taken from John
Steinbeck's update of the Cain and
Abel story, Warner agrees immediately,
and approves a budget twice that of
Waterfront. "Cast who you want," says
the studio boss.

Kazan's self-confidence is
unhindered now. He regards *East of
Eden* as "a very personal film, one of
the most personal I ever made, much
more so than *On the Waterfront*. I was
very like Cal, so *East of Eden* was for me
a kind of self-defense. It was about
people not understanding me." And
Kazan's first instinct is to think of
Brando and Montgomery Clift for the
two brothers—this is around the time
when Brando walks out of the
Waterfront screening without a word.
Brando says that he is busy—at thirty,
he was also too old, not too say too
solid, too bulky, to match the essential adolescent in Cal. Still, there is some
sense of repayment or rebuke as Kazan makes it his business to discover
someone else for the part—James Dean, six years younger than Brando, a
great deal less secure and already famously difficult.

No one doubts but that Dean has grown up enthralled by Brando. He is
from the Midwest, too, from a farm and a small town in Indiana. He can
claim graver parental problems than affected Marlon: his father left the
family when Dean was a child, and Dean is never certain that this man is even
his true father. Just as Brando the young actor was an intense, greedy student
of others, so Dean has a fixation on Brando. And the older man does not like
it. They are at the same parties sometimes, and Brando has a way of ignoring
the clinging, adoring Dean, or of telling him off.

"Once he showed up at a party," writes Brando, "and I saw him take off
his jacket, roll it into a ball and throw it on the floor." Nearly every woman
who has spent time with Brando has noted his wayward treatment of his own
clothes, and picked up after him. But now he lectures Dean on tidiness and
doesn't seem to see the joke.

"Another time, I told him I thought he was foolish to try to copy me as
an actor. 'Jimmy, you have to be who you are, not who I am. You mustn't try
to copy me. Emulate the best aspects of yourself.' I said it was a dead-end
street to try to be somebody else." Yet there are so many friends who have
been dazzled, if alarmed, by Brando's constant need to be other and
imaginary people. It has been noted already that, even in film, Brando does

not have his own voice, his own style and self—like John Wayne, William Holden or Gary Cooper. Some admire that versatility, yet some already have noticed the absence, the emptiness, at the center. (To this day, when impressionists "do" Brando, they pick on his scenes and voices. But if they "do" Wayne or Cooper or Cagney, they do the general sound of the voice. No one does Dean— because he had so few films, or because he became sacred?

Kazan is not alone in saying that Dean is going to be remarkable in *East of Eden*. At the same time, the director has discovered what he calls a really "sick kid," such a figure of sexual insecurity and neurotic instincts that Kazan and Julie Harris have to nurse him along through *Eden*. Whereas Brando has never required such tenderness. Brando is stronger, steadier, more secure than Dean—which does not mean that Brando is unhurt by the comparisons. For the hint is there that Dean may be more mercurial, more emotional, more touched by vagrant genius—if genius has to be a vagrant quality. Kazan has remarked that Dean has a "very poetic face…You feel so sorry for him when you see him in close-up." In addition, he says that "his body was more expressive, actually, in free movement, than Brando's." Take away the face and the body, and what have you got? In a word, you have a younger rival who has won away your own mentor.

That loss coincides with two other things. Brando discovers that the several schemes his father has undertaken with Marlon's money have been disastrous. The money is gone, and it never comes back. In suits taken against various people, it emerges that something like $120,000 of the money has been squandered on mining and cattle-ranching schemes. That is certainly a warning against the way he has been operating, but it is also fuel to his growing resentment about money. It accounts for his insistence on getting his money up front on *On the Waterfront*, which in turn sets off a grievous loss of profit participation. In other words, Brando's emotional immaturity begins to add to his steady concern over money, something that will look increasingly ugly. Famously indifferent to "business," he will become awfully money-grubbing.

Marlon Sr. and Dodie visit the set of *On the Waterfront*. She does not look well; she looks older than her fifty-seven years. Then in March, she collapses and never comes out of a coma. She dies on the morning of March 31, with Marlon at her bedside. He takes a lock of her hair and a ring from her finger. "It was about five A.M. on a spring

The New Guy
James Dean, wrote Elia Kazan in *A Life*, "dropped his voice to a cathedral hush when he talked about Marlon." But though Kazan admired Dean's natural gift, he felt the younger actor was not as skilled as Brando, who had benefitted from his training in New York.

Meet the Parents
While making *Waterfront*, Brando shows his father and mother the set-up (above), attended by the producer, Sam Spiegel (in the dark coat)—already dreaming of Best Picture.

Happy to Have It
Marlon Brando shows few doubts over appearing to pick up his Oscar (right) for *On the Waterfront* at the Pantages Theatre in Hollywood, March 30, 1955.

morning in Pasadena, and it seemed as if everything in nature had been imbued with her spirit: the birds, the leaves, the flowers and especially the wind, all seemed to reflect it. She had given me a love of nature and animals, and the night sky, and a sense of closeness to the earth. I felt she was with me there, outside the hospital, and it helped me get through the loss."

But he talks a lot about feeling alone, about having nothing in his life with enough meaning. He may feel trapped with the father he has less reason to admire. It is soon after the death of his mother that he nearly marries the French girl, Josanne. An actual, and disastrous, marriage is not that far away. He makes, or is drawn into, disastrous career decisions. And James Dean is delivering a performance that some people will say surpasses Brando. Then Dean is killed, far too early, and the impact of his three films is inextricably caught up in a teenage cult that is more intense than the mood Brando commanded a few years earlier. Why should he not feel rueful or jealous?

On the Waterfront opens in July 1954, and it receives enormous praise. A few months later, it gets twelve Academy Award nominations. Brando will profess uncertainty as to whether or not to attend the event. Being driven to the ceremony, wearing a tuxedo, he thinks of backing away. But he attends, and even engages in some pre-scripted badinage with host Bob Hope.

On the Waterfront wins eight Oscars, including Picture, Director, Screenplay and Supporting Actress. In the category of Supporting Actor, not unreasonably, *Waterfront* has three nominees—Steiger, Malden and Cobb—but they all lose to Edmond O'Brien for *The Barefoot Contessa*. As for Actor, Brando is competing with Bing Crosby in *The Country Girl*, Humphrey Bogart in *The Caine Mutiny*, James Mason in *A Star Is Born* and Dan O'Herlihy in Luis Buñuel's *Adventures of Robinson Crusoe*.

Bette Davis is presenting that Oscar, and when it goes to Brando he says "I can't remember what I was going to say for the life of me. I don't think ever in my life that so many people were so directly responsible for my being so very, very happy." He looks young, awkward and sincere, and if only because of the profound inaccuracy of what he says it is likely that he is speaking from the heart. It is one of the last glimpses of that carefree Marlon Brando.

Carlo Fiore tells a strange story of this Brando. It occurs in Los Angeles, on a flat roof in Laurel Canyon, where Brando is engaged in strenuous lovemaking with a Latina woman. She is crying out in passion, and Brando urges her on until she screams in the echo-ridden space of the canyon, "Oh, fuck me, Marlon Brando!"

He stops. He claps a hand over her mouth and hisses, "Don't use my name!" The neurotic celebrity has overtaken the human animal.

MOVIE STAR

Having cost a little under $900,000, *On the Waterfront* grosses $6 million in its first run. That is astonishing success for so harsh a story, and it marks the beginning of a period in which Marlon Brando is not just an audacious actor with a cult following but a genuine movie star and a box-office draw who can shape projects to his own will. Some trade research puts Brando high up in public popularity, and as if to mark that he embarks on a series of pictures that he despises for being crowd-pleasers. Thus a disconcerting paradox sets in: Brando is not too far from enjoying the love of the general public—after years of limited, cult status and widespread ridicule because of his mumbling and his studied incoherence. He seems to be relaxing, having fun   dressing up and making faces in several lightweight projects. But in truth, he is sinking into a kind of wretchedness in which he hates himself as much as he does the film business.

So it's worth stressing that he might have been doing more plays in New York (where Kazan directs *Cat on a Hot Tin Roof* in 1955, with Ben Gazzara in the lead). He might have been building his craft with John Gielgud and Paul Scofield in London. He might even have set himself up as an actor-producer on a par with Burt Lancaster, say, who makes *Sweet Smell of Success* in 1957, or Henry Fonda, who does *Twelve Angry Men* the same year. Instead, Brando begins to make pictures almost in a spirit of vengeance against a system he deplores. But the greatest affront to that system is to step outside it, to do something as different and challenging as *Streetcar* or *Waterfront*. There are actors coming along who admit a huge debt to Brando—like Paul Newman—who will embark on film careers that are so much more enterprising. I do not mean to say that Brando would have found the will or the nerve to do *The Hustler, Hud, Cool Hand Luke* or, years later, *The Verdict, Nobody's Fool* or even *Road to Perdition*.

But there is a time in Newman's early career when he can hardly credit being a rival to Brando. And Paul Newman is only nine months younger than Marlon Brando.

So it's telling, in 1954, that Brando will complain mildly at having been "snookered" into a deal with Fox to do two pictures. His agent, Jay Kanter, shows him the contract, but Brando presents himself as someone happier to sign than read all that small print. So it is that Brando finds himself announced by Darryl Zanuck as playing in *The Egyptian*, a wide-screen biblical epic, with Victor Mature, Gene Tierney and Jean Simmons backing the central romance between Brando (as Sinuhe, a doctor) and Bella Darvi (as a whore). Darvi is also the discovery, and mistress, of Darryl Zanuck.

Brando finds the script risible and so on the eve of production he leaves Los Angeles for New York. Within days, Fox files a $2 million suit for breach of contract. Brando claims to be exhausted and in dire need of regular consultations with Bela Mittelmann. Fox is skeptical and tough-minded: they allege that Brando has left reading *The Egyptian* until far too late. But a compromise is reached: Brando must pay half the cost of delay and must then agree to play Napoleon Bonaparte in another film, *Desirée*. Thus is history manipulated in Hollywood. In addition, he must do a second film for Fox at some date. Brando is in a corner, short of money after his father's deals, and so he agrees to the new contract and will do *Desirée* for $125,000. (*The Egyptian* is recast with newcomer Edmund Purdom, and takes its place among the silliest films ever made.)

Desirée cannot claim to be much more respectable, though there is a merry, flirtatious air between Brando and Jean Simmons, playing the seamstress who wins the emperor's eye. The director is Henry Koster, who strikes Brando as being more interested in uniforms than in people or history. Nevertheless, here is Stanley Kowalski trying to be as suave as Charles Boyer, and with veteran beauty Merle Oberon as his Josephine. It is somewhere between a throwback and a throwaway, but to the innocent public it seems adorable to have Brando doing Bonaparte. The film is a big hit, at which the great actor shrugs at finding contempt confirmed so easily.

The next venture does better still. Samuel Goldwyn and Joseph L. Mankiewicz invite him to take on Sky Masterson in their picture of *Guys and Dolls*— a singing, dancing role. Mankiewicz points out that the two of them had never done

Desirée
If you tickle me, you're dead: The very straight faces of Jean Simmons and Marlon Brando in a publicity pose for *Desirée*—a film in which you wear the costumes and act like history.

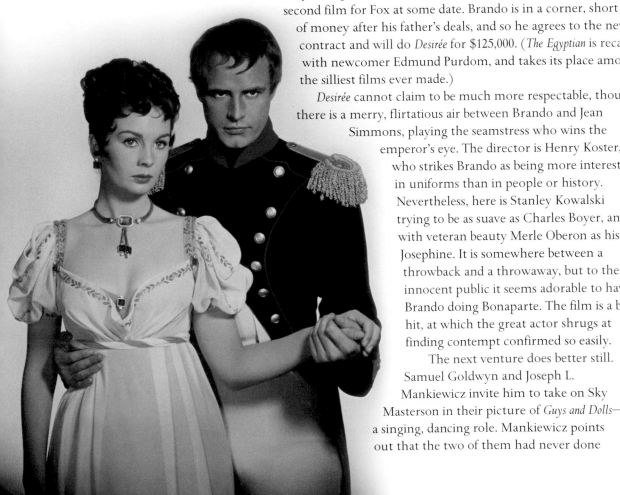

Joker Joked
Choreographer Michael Kidd trumps Brando on the set of *Guys and Dolls* when the actor's chronic gum habit had already spoiled several takes.

Shakespeare before, and that turned out well. So why not a musical? Brando will pick up $200,000 this time, along with the renewed resentment of Frank Sinatra, who wanted the role of Masterson for himself and has to settle for Nathan Detroit.

The public at large is charmed by the husky, nasal way in which Brando sings "A Woman in Love." The scenes with Jean Simmons, as Sister Sarah, are both funny and erotic—there is a great prolonged kiss, with Sarah apparently in a trance, until she wipes the cocksure grin off Sky's face (and sets Brando's jowls quivering) with a mighty slap. And Brando even goes into a kind of elephantine shimmy in the great dance number "Luck Be a Lady." Many observe how fleshy Brando looks. The heavy drape jacket he wears is meant to conceal burgeoning hips. And truly, he looks too angelic to be a gangster. But Mankiewicz's film gets away with its own lack of musical touch. Instead, this film opts for stressing the characters in the lead roles and the cheek of having Brando and Simmons sing the Frank Loesser songs. (Looking on the bright side, Goldwyn's wife, Frances, opines that Brando sounds like a young Fred Astaire.) *Guys and Dolls* proves very expensive, but it grosses $13 million and is the big hit of 1955.

Is it challenge, or further evasion, that Brando now elects to play Sakini, the Japanese interpreter in the military comedy *Teahouse of the August Moon*? The film is adapted by John Patrick from his own play, and Brando has been impressed by David Wayne as Sakini on stage. MGM is happy to go along with his request. It's another good salary, though Brando takes a touch less to help the picture get made. In return, he is given director approval (for the first time), and he exercises that privilege by approving the mild-mannered and none-too-vigorous Daniel Mann. Some say it's a director too meek to interfere with him.

His co-star in *Teahouse* is Glenn Ford, a very deft actor, but an old-fashioned man who hardly bothers to conceal his hostility to Brando. The shooting becomes a battle between two artful scene-stealers, with Brando teasing and tormenting Ford off-camera. But though Brando can feel superior to Ford, like a playful bee darting in and out of his staid bloom, in fact Ford is exactly the kind of actor who has a set persona that works very well on screen in a wide variety of genres. Ford regards Brando as a vain showoff, while Brando treats Ford like a stick-in-the-mud. But Ford's simple presence actually contributes to a mass of good films (*Gilda*, *The Big Heat*, *Blackboard Jungle*, *3:10 to Yuma*) in a way Brando will never manage.

One other appeal in *Teahouse* for Brando is the chance to work in Japan, and to make some fun of American crassness in Asian eyes. On the way to Tokyo, he makes a small, private tour of the Pacific, in part because he is toying with the idea of a documentary about United Nations work in the area, to be made by his own, recently formed company, Pennebaker. It's during this trip that Brando discovers Bali and has one of those epiphanies—like the moment when he luxuriated in the fragrant fields of Sicily. Here is the Brando who will one day have his own Pacific island.

"Before tourists polluted their culture, Balinese women didn't wear anything over their breasts, although if you encountered one on a street she usually covered herself up out of courtesy, not that she thought there was anything wrong with being bare-breasted, but as a show of respect. The women had beautiful bodies, and I kept trying to persuade them to be less respectful. Sitting in a stream with my feet braced against a boulder and water splashing over my shoulders, or looking down river at a group of naked Balinese women bathing, I thought nothing in life could be more pleasant than this. A sailor I met had jumped ship in Bali and decided to spend the rest of his life there. I understood why."

Teahouse of the August Moon is another hit, and that justifies Brando's demand for $300,000 to make *Sayonara*, with Joshua Logan

He Sings! He Dances!
For his big singing and dancing number in *Guys and Dolls*, "Luck, Be a Lady Tonight" (left), Brando required some one hundred takes. The studio didn't care about the expense, figuring the come-on of Marlon singing would be box-office gold. That's Stubby Kaye (as Nicely Nicely Johnson) in the light jacket.

No *Tea* Party
In *Teahouse of the August Moon*, Brando and Glenn Ford (below) blatantly tried to upstage each other. This scene suggests an uneasy truce. The mismatched pair also battled over cookies and politics.

Teahouse Tryst

As with *Teahouse*, Brando saw *Sayonara* as a chance to dispel American stereotypes of Asians. But critics (and the studio, to judge from this poster) focused on the romance between Brando and Miiko Taka. The film won Supporting Actor and Actress Oscars for Red Buttons and Miyoshi Umeki.

directing. It's the story of a Korean War pilot who falls in love with a Japanese woman (Miiko Taka). It's taken from a James Michener story, with a script by Paul Osborn. But Brando has script approval, and on a whim he asks for his character to be made a southerner, thus requiring an exaggerated southern drawl.

Joshua Logan musters his patience to engage in prolonged discussions with Brando, in which the actor ruminates over many things. Vanity and self-indulgence have had an unfortunate effect on the legendary mumbling, for now Brando tends to spout and pontificate, invariably using extra-long words to display his abilities. For Logan, it is one of the ordeals on *Sayonara*:

"Marlon talked interminably. When he gets rhetorical it's like a tapeworm. He wanted to make sure that he was going to be safe, that we would back him up. In most stories, he told us, the Asians are treated as second-class citizens; he wouldn't be party to any such stereotype. Again, I said we would make the changes and he could read them for himself. He left, saying he would like to think about it and maybe have another meeting. He was perfectly right, except that I wondered if he would ever listen to anyone else talk but himself."

The man was a problem, but the actor is there still. For the key scene in which Brando's character proposes to the Japanese woman, the scene had been written and rewritten. Logan feels it requires great delicacy, but lo and behold when they shoot it Brando comes on like a gangster haranguing his moll. A furious argument develops between actor and director.

"What the hell do you mean?" Brando roars. "I've had to do one tough scene in every picture I've made. They want it."

Logan remonstrates and says this approach is juvenile. "Marlon, who was ready to say something louder to top me, suddenly made one of those miraculous changes of his from high to reverse without going through neutral." So he walks on the set and plays it perfectly, the way Logan has asked. And this is a performance that will win Brando his fifth best actor nomination (he lost to Alec Guinness in *The Bridge on the River Kwai*).

It is during *Sayonara* that Truman Capote persuades Brando to give him an interview for a *New Yorker* profile. The actor is wary, and he thinks he's speaking off the record. But then the unscrupulous Capote uses the worst or the most naive things he has said and easily paints a portrait of Brando as a wordy chump:

"Have you ever been analyzed? I was afraid of it at first. Afraid it might destroy the impulses that made me creative, an artist. A sensitive person receives fifty impressions where somebody else may only get seven. Sensitive people are so vulnerable; they're so easily brutalized and hurt because they are sensitive. The more sensitive you are, the more certain you are to be brutalized."

No one questions that this is Marlon: wordy, ruminative, tender but self-pitying, earnest and very young. Capote's accuracy is the unkindest cut of all. Brando's trust has been exploited. He digs in harder against the media and the cruel ways of show business.

Sayonara is such a hit that Brando's ten percent of the profits brings in close to another $1 million, in addition to his $300,000 salary. But at this point Twentieth Century-Fox comes back with the reminder that Brando owes them another picture still. They offer *The Young Lions,* taken from Irwin Shaw's best-selling novel, but it turns out that Brando will have to take a pay cut to do it. Still, he prevails upon director Edward Dmytryk and screenwriter Edward Anhalt to change his character, Christian Diestl. In the book, Christian is a German officer who becomes a Nazi; in the film, he is a "good" German who is led to appreciate the criminal nature of Naziism.

Brando goes Aryan ash blond for the part, and his bulk is somewhat hidden by the uniform. But in truth, he is outplayed by Montgomery Clift, as the victimized Jewish soldier, Noah Ackerman. They are fellow Nebraskans. They have been uneasy friends, and untouchably brilliant actors. And Brando has occasionally volunteered to do all he can to help the unstable Clift. But Clift may be the more touching actor, given the right role. *The Young Lions* is so strangely constructed that Clift and Brando (and Dean Martin) only come together for the last scene. They never really work together, and Clift is often disapproving of Brando's attempts to make the German officer Christ-like. But Clift is so sick, so dependent on drink and drugs, as to be near his end. Thus Brando will survive his most obvious rivals—Clift and Dean—and yet seem stranded by their loss. And in his way of thinking, is it possible that the most sensitive are doomed to perish young?

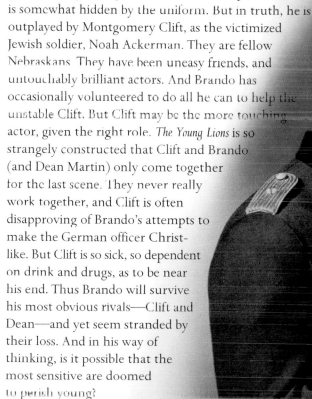

Nazi Dude
Even great actors respond to the thrill of dressing up in uniform—Brando, with blonde rinse and May Britt, as a young German officer in *the Young Lions*.

Auteur
1955–1960

WEDLOCK

One day in November 1955, Brando is having lunch in the Paramount commissary with Eva Marie Saint. They are friendly still from *On the Waterfront*. He is about to leave for Japan to make *Teahouse of the August Moon*; she is at Paramount to do a picture with Bob Hope, *That Certain Feeling*. Then a young woman at another table is introduced to Brando. Has he noticed her and asked, or is the meeting at her instigation? No one quite remembers, though later it will be said she was aiming for him. She says her name is Anna Kashfi; and she has a modest role in the Spencer Tracy picture *The Mountain*. She is beautiful, slender and very dark. She says she is Indian. Marlon is immediately attracted.

She says she was born in Calcutta in 1934, the daughter of an architect, Devi Kashfi, and a woman named Selma Ghose. It is not quite clear if her parents were ever married. But when Anna is a small child, she says, her mother marries again, to William Patrick O'Callaghan, a British citizen working for the railways. In time, she goes back to Britain with her mother and stepfather and lives in Wales. There is some time in Italy, and later she has tried to be a model in London before coming to Hollywood.

Marlon telephones her a day or so after the first meeting. They go out together a few times, though Kashfi will later claim that she didn't yet know who Marlon Brando was. They become lovers, and for a time he is infatuated with her, making love at every opportunity. Later on, she will observe that Marlon is a

Mother and Child Reunion

Six-year-old Christian Devi Brando leaps into the arms of his mother, Anna Kashfi, in December 1964. A week earlier, she had temporarily lost custody of him to Brando.

selfish, vain lover, happier talking to his "noble tool" than to the woman who is receiving it. On the other hand, he seems to make some effort to be faithful to her and is plainly entranced by her Indian appearance.

He goes to Japan. A few months pass. The relationship is not forsaken, though, and it gets a strange reinforcement when, in the spring of 1956, Kashfi is hospitalized in Los Angeles with a serious case of tuberculosis. For three months, she resides at the City of Hope Hospital, with Brando a regular visitor. He begins to tell her about his life, about his mother. He gives Anna jewelry that belonged to Dodie. He tells her, "It's better she's dead. If she'd lived, I could never have loved you. She wouldn't have let me go."

When Anna is released, Brando sets her up in an apartment close to where his father lives. Marlon Sr. is a bond the son cannot break. Despite the business misdealings, the father still oversees Marlon's business and financial affairs. Anna Kashfi witnesses Senior's arrogance and temper, and she has to endure his fierce scrutiny of her own expenditures. Like most of Marlon's friends, the father is suspicious and disapproving of Anna. While Brando is shooting *The Young Lions* in Europe, he employs his father to keep watch on Anna as she dines occasionally with the actor Curt Jurgens. (Is this the first sign of sexual jealousy in Brando?)

The love affair is no longer as intense—Rita Moreno has come back into his life as an urgent rival. But then Anna announces that she is pregnant, and Marlon talks about actually marrying her. Carlo Fiore urges an abortion—not the first in Brando's romantic career. But something about this relationship digs deeper. On October 11, 1957, at the Eagle Rock home of his aunt, Marlon and Anna are married, with the bride wearing a green and gold sari. Only then does Brando realize he hasn't thought of a honeymoon. So they drive around Los Angeles until Jay Kanter gives them his house for a night, and then they go to Palm Springs to be with Westerns author Louis L'Amour, whom Kashfi knows.

There is never a honeymoon. The news of the wedding brings skeletons out of many cupboards. In Cardiff, William Patrick O'Callaghan tells reporters that Anna is his daughter. She had been raised in India, but she isn't Indian at all. He says her name is Joan O'Callaghan, and it turns out one film studio had paid her as "Joanna O'Callaghan"—the name she had used when entering the United States. Has the great actor and the chronic practical joker, the guy always phoning you up and pretending to be someone else, been hoodwinked?

The furor will never be settled. But it should be said that, despite private assurances of confidence, Brando is one of those who hire detectives and researchers in an attempt to sort out the matter. Though the couple moves into a new house, 12900 Mulholland Drive (a place built for Howard Hughes), that home will last far longer than the marriage. Brando feels humiliated and there are many press reports of a breakup, long before the birth of Christian Devi Brando in May 1958.

There is a brief interlude in which Brando is in love with his child, but soon he is parading a new conquest—the Eurasian actress France Nuyen—in front of Anna. In September 1958, in the Mulholland house, the couple's Japanese maid, Sako, drowns while swimming in the pool. Anna is unable to save her. Confused messages suggest that it is Anna who has died. Brando rushes home and, according to Anna, is filled with dismay when he finds her still alive. That day she takes Christian and leaves the house. She hears later that Marlon is threatening to drown himself in the same pool. Whereupon she drives back to the house and shouts out, "Jump, you son of a bitch! Jump!"

It is the start of prolonged court battles over the custody of Christian. Anna's own career as an actress peters out. In 1979, she will publish a scandalous book, *Brando for Breakfast*, but she is seldom in good health. Even at the time of her marriage, there are those who feel that Anna believed she was Indian, or was too lost in fantasy to know what was true. Winning Brando has been a major event in her drama, and now that is over. She takes to drink and drugs, and becomes a relentless opponent of Brando, vindictive, inventive and torturing. Christian is torn between the two of them in ghastly ways. He hardly knows where he lives. But in 1960, Brando marries Movita. They rarely live together, but she will have two children by him—a son, Sergio, or Miko (born in October 1960), and a daughter, Rebecca (born in September 1966). It should be added that there is significant doubt as to whether Marlon is actually father to these two children, though from time to time he supports them.

When he shoots *Mutiny on the Bounty*, he will seduce Tarita Tumi Teriipaia, with whom he later lives as a common-law wife. She is the mother of their son, Teihotu (born in May 1963), and a daughter, Cheyenne (born in February 1970).

This does not exhaust the list of long-term associations or children. But it is enough to justify some

CUSTODY OF CHRISTIAN

Brando and Christian enter a Santa Monica court in 1972, for yet another round of custody talks.

The court battles between Brando and Anna Kashfi over Christian went on and on, with incalculable effect on the child. Many people observed that he tried to relate to nannies and nurses, but those jobs were always changing. Essentially the courts reckoned that Brando should have custody of the boy—Kashfi's instability was apparent, she was not earning, and she had epilepsy. But in December 1964, having only just survived a drug overdose, Kashfi broke into the Brando house and took the boy. The actor and private detectives pursued them to a hotel, and showed a court order calling for Christian's return. The next judge in the case decreed that Kashfi could see her own son only in the presence of a lawyer. Then Christian was put in the care of his aunt, Fran (Marlon's sister), but she was obliged to report that the boy was very disturbed. This pattern of turmoil and change never let up.

Now I Get It
Tarita, who had never heard of Brando before he arrived in Tahiti to shoot *Mutiny on the Bounty*, checks out a publicity poster of her husband at a Hollywood theater.

Hapless Hunk
Brando poses for a publicity shot in September 1952 (right). Hollywood's newest screen god was already a reluctant movie star.

comment on the man addicted to women yet averse to relationship. And just as one would not place all the blame on Marlon's shoulders for things done by his son, Christian, so it seems self-pitying and irrelevant for anyone to argue that Marlon's personal chaos is the responsibility of his mother and father. Nor can one simply conclude that in studying an actor the personal life should be kept marginal.

To say that is to compromise Brando's true worth as an actor. His power has always been sexual; it is the breath he inhales that separates his phrasing; it is in the deep sympathy of his movements. From *Streetcar* to *Last Tango in Paris*, Brando has offered himself as our sexual outlaw, as a kind of willful pioneer on that dangerous frontier. So it is proper to say that in life and on screen Brando has denied himself—or fled from—prolonged relationships (as in marriage) or lasting familial ties. One may say that *The Godfather* is different, that Vito Corleone is a family man, in love with his sons. That is true, but only on a basis that eliminates their critical questioning. That may be one reason among many why the part so appealed to Brando, and fulfilled him.

The facts speak clearly—and there are sadder stories to come. There is no need to moralize, but every need to point out the detail and the dread of his great loneliness. It makes it easier to grasp the wish to succeed as an actor that Marlon Brando exists in such failure as a man.

ACTOR, AUTEUR

In Marlon Brando's autobiography, *One-Eyed Jacks* is dealt with in two-and-a-half pages—in life, Paramount must have yearned for some similar economy. It was, in its day, the great actor taking on that stalwart and reliable genre, the Western; it was also the most vital actor of his time becoming a movie director. More than that, the psychological premise of the film is painfully applicable to Brando himself in its study of the love-hate relationship between the Kid (Brando) and Dad Longworth (Karl Malden). They are fellow outlaws, until Dad abandons the Kid to years of jail and rides away to another town where he will be sheriff and stepfather to a lovely girl. Here was the prospect of a fascinating star exploring his own depths— and there are more than hints in the surviving film of what might have been. Yet the two-and-a-half pages in Brando's autobiography reflect the bizarre mixture of lassitude and intensity in Brando, and the way in which a six-month shoot and an absurd final budget of close to $6 million could be wiped away with this:

"When we got back to Hollywood, someone said we had enough footage to make a movie six or eight hours long. I started editing it, but pretty soon got sick of it and turned the job over to someone else. When he had finished, Paramount said it didn't like my version of the story: I'd had everybody in the picture lie except Karl Malden. The studio cut the movie to pieces and made him a liar, too. By then I was bored with the whole project and walked away from it."

Whereas Brando is openly scornful of the box-office pictures he makes in the late '50s, he nurses the idea of a Western to be made for his own company, Pennebaker. The Truman Capote interview makes fun of the project and its vivid, alternate titles. One idea was to make *The Count of Monte Cristo* as a Western. Brando hires Niven Busch (the author of *Duel in the Sun*) to write a script, but Busch, a Hollywood veteran and a very practical storyteller, is bewildered by Brando's vague ideas about bringing nature into the film, and his complete unawareness of story and structure.

Meanwhile, a producer, Frank Rosenberg, has bought the rights to a new Western novel, *The Authentic Death of Hendry Jones*, by Charles Neider. It is a reworking of the Billy the Kid–Pat Garrett story, transposed from New Mexico to northern California, and a tale of youthful wildness and middle-aged sobriety. Rosenberg enlisted an up and coming screenwriter, Sam Peckinpah, to make a script from the novel. Peckinpah (then thirty-two) does a good job, and Rosenberg—having heard of the actor's desire to do a Western—sends it to Brando. In a couple of weeks, Brando declares he loves it. Pennebaker buys the rights and the script for $150,000 and a deal is made with Paramount for a picture to cost $1.8 million. There are meetings and the idea is proposed that another relative newcomer, Stanley Kubrick (then twenty-nine), will direct. Brando approves this hiring after he has seen Kubrick's film *The Killing*. But Kubrick says that he wants to bring in his own writer, so Peckinpah is dropped and Calder Willingham enters the scene.

In hindsight, it is recollected with awe that Brando feels the Peckinpah script is ready to shoot. Kubrick and Willingham raise doubts, which turn into prolonged discussions at Brando's house—script conferences forever interrupted by chess matches, music, drinking, the viewing of pornographic movies and Brando's urge to talk about anything except the picture. Willingham writes some pages, but no one is excited. Guy Trosper takes over, with no greater success. The impatient

Kubrick (he has other projects pressing, including Vladimir Nabokov's *Lolita*) presses for action. He feels that the Longworth character requires a very strong actor, someone who can stand up to Brando. He wants Spencer Tracy. But Brando sighs and says no good, he's already hired—and guaranteed $300,000—for Karl Malden, his old pal. Kubrick thinks Malden is too pliant for the role. And so a day comes when Kubrick announces, with regret, that he feels he no longer knows where the project is going, and escapes.

And it is then that Marlon Brando decides that perhaps he had better direct it himself. He will say that he has been forced into directing to save the picture, but others fancy he has always had this result in mind. The worst truth may be that both estimates are correct: that he has meant to direct, but does not realize that. This is not good preparation for directing.

Of course, these events overlap with the Kashfi marriage and divorce, and just as Brando had extra reasons for being upset, so he had great need of money and he would be paid $500,000 by Paramount for acting in and directing the picture. Moreover, his closest associates notice an increasing divide in his nature: taking the project immensely seriously and then laughing at how he is doing it for the money; veering from exhilaration to depression or a Buddhist calm; getting in shape for the picture, but then eating enormous double meals. And something else: having to make up his mind (for filmmaking is one damn

Roll 'Em!

When Paramount executives showed up on the set of *One-Eyed Jacks* to complain about cost overruns, director Brando hurled obscenities at them. On weekends, he would casually fly to New York to see women.

decision after another) and yet clinging to the appealing doubt of never quite making up his mind—so that, late in the day, the story might go in any of several different directions. Don't rule out the possibility that being a director, deciding, deciding, deciding, is a true agony for him. As hard as being steady or consistent with one person— anyone—from day to day.

As *One-Eyed Jacks* begins shooting, late in 1958, it has already come close to exhausting its $1.8 million budget. But the shoot will stretch over six months, with location work in Mexico, Death Valley and the Monterey peninsula, before returning to the Paramount lot.

Brando has changed the novel's ending: now, it is the Kid who will kill Dad Longworth. But variations stay with him throughout and even in the final version of the picture there is a suggestion that Dad has shot his own stepdaughter, the Kid's beloved.

For that role, Frank Rosenberg goes to Mexico and finds Pina Pellicer, a notably thin and very nervous young woman who has just played Anne Frank on the stage. On location, it is inevitable that she and Brando have an affair, but Pellicer is unusually delicate and there are those who regret hearing Brando talking to her about suicide. Only a few years later, in Mexico, Pina Pellicer will kill herself. And all she can observe on *One-Eyed Jacks* is the craziness of Hollywood and Brando's sexual use of just about every woman in the cast—including Katy Jurado—to say nothing of occasional visitors like France Nuyen.

There are many stories of the sexual indulgence, of eating binges and of the director's helplessness with his new medium. He spends most of one day on the Monterey shore, waiting for the right wave to appear in the background, but hardly grasping that it will be gone before he can film it. He spends hours rewriting the script, and then urges the actors to improvise. He keeps players waiting weeks on end, so that their salaries are far greater than they might have been. He is forever adding and deleting sequences. And he's eating so much that his costumes have to be elasticized—no matter that he looks like the beefiest person ever to emerge from five years in a Sonora prison!

But the postproduction is more painful still. It lasts from June 1959 to March 1961, and involves Brando in the dire task of having to make up his mind with over 200 miles of film. At first, he seems to think that he can take fragments from different takes to build an assembly. But they do not match. It is as if he has never really understood how a film is made. He finds the days

Sweet Revenge
Brando has sheriff Karl Malden on his knees in this scene from *One-Eyed Jacks*, but Malden later gets his revenge, with a nasty horsewhip.

KING OF SOCCER

• In June of 1958, the Brazilian national soccer team beats Sweden to capture the World Cup. Fans around the world are captivated by a young player named Edson Arantes do Nascimento—soon to be known simply as Pelé, King of Soccer.

Marlon and Joanne

Brando (in a famous snakeskin jacket) and Joanne Woodward (in a scene from *The Fugitive Kind*) had dated briefly in 1953. By the time of the film, she was married to Paul Newman, and a new mom. "I hated working with Marlon," she said later, "because he was not there, he was somewhere else."

in the editing room a nightmare—this is the man who has boasted to Truman Capote that he has only a seven-minute attention span. He has never had to work like this, and he can hardly escape his own failure.

Literally, he reaches an eight-hour cut, and reckons it is plausible. Finally, he shows a four-and-a-half-hour version to Frank Rosenberg and the exasperated producer says it's still just an assembly of footage. In the end, there is mercy. Paramount takes the picture away from him—onlookers believe Brando is relieved by this intervention. He is left able to sneer at the 141-minute version that is finally released. And in later years—as directors' cuts become fashionable—he is guaranteed superiority by the way Paramount has dumped all the excess footage for the silver nitrate. There is an audience for the picture, led by curiosity, but it cannot overcome the prodigious costs on making, completing and marketing the picture. He has never directed again.

But *One-Eyed Jacks* is not hopeless or a bad joke. The settings are beautiful. The supporting cast is filled with good performances from Ben Johnson, Slim Pickens, Timothy Carey and Elisha Cook. Much of the dialogue is pungent and fresh—and often it seems to be the improvised passages. Some sequences are shot and cut with real distinction. And, most interesting of all, there is a great subject at the core of the film.

The Kid and Rio are bank robbers. But after one job they are tracked down by a Mexican posse and trapped with one horse. They draw lots to decide which one shall ride off for fresh horses—but the Kid arranges this in such a way (it is very deliberately shot) that he will be the loser. Dad escapes and never comes back. The Kid goes to jail. He escapes after five years and tracks down Dad to a coastal town in northern California. He plans to seduce Dad's stepdaughter, rob the bank in his town and kill Dad. And more or less that's how the picture ends.

But there are hints of so much more: of the Kid in love with the Dad he hates, of a Kid as self-destructive as he is vengeful. That character study is not explored, though there are scenes where Brando is filled with seething disquiet. Was there ever a chance of it being a more blatant statement about his mixed feelings for his father—or for Elia Kazan? We can't say. As you watch it, you know the film is lost. It is still too long, too imprecise. But then you ask yourself what if . . . what if the troubled feelings of this actor had been able to inspire and retain the full support of such talents as Sam Peckinpah and Stanley Kubrick? What then? And what if Kazan had played Dad Longworth? It's harder to forget that version than it is to recall the film actually released.

MILLION-DOLLAR MAN

One reason for doing *The Fugitive Kind* is as an escape from the dilemmas of editing *One-Eyed Jacks*. Another is $1 million. The film has begun life as a Tennessee Williams play, *Orpheus Descending*, a perilously poetic tale in which Val Xavier, a used-up blues musician, with guitar and snakeskin jacket, comes to a small, bigoted southern town and falls for the sheriff's wife, Lady Torrance. It has played on Broadway, in 1957, with Cliff Robertson and Maureen Stapleton, but by far its most successful presentation has been in Italy with Anna Magnani in the lead role. It is she who urges Williams to make a film script out if it, and it is she who has a great desire to have Brando as her co-star.

Magnani is fifty-one in 1960 (she could be Marlon's mother, just), but she has won the Oscar in 1955 in *The Rose Tattoo* and she has achieved her own strange domination of the English language. So the film is set up, but the production is in such need of Brando—for the box office—that he gets $1 million, and lets it be known that he is only doing the picture to pay Anna Kashfi's divorce settlement. No one in American pictures has been paid $1 million, up front, before. Elizabeth Taylor claims that novelty a little later with *Cleopatra*, but only because Brando's salary is deliberately misreported to divert attention, and outrage. Magnani and the director Sidney Lumet receive $125,000 each.

Magnani arrives in New York and is Tallulah Bankhead again: older, very experienced, sexually aggressive, challenging—exactly the one kind of woman Marlon Brando flinches from. He becomes inordinately respectful and considerate, as if she were an old lady instead of just an older woman. He makes a few remarks about her looks. For reason, Magnani is known as "La Lupa" (the Wolf), for she is fierce, intimidating, not too far from ugly—that is her kind of attractiveness. The two stars get on very badly, and the matter is exacerbated by the fact that Maureen Stapleton (an old friend of Marlon's) is playing a supporting part in the film.

The film proves a commercial disaster and it is said to be the first Brando picture that loses money. So be it. It is also a very moving work in which the ill-fitting leads (with Joanne Woodward) bring astonishing life to Williams' shaky poetics. As shot by Boris Kaufman (the cameraman from *On the Waterfront*) in vivid black-and-white, it is a curiosity well worth tracking down.

LUNCH SIT-IN

• Black college students protest segregation in Greensboro, North Carolina by taking seats at a white-only lunch counter. The white waitresses refuse to serve them, but lunch counter sit-ins spread to other Southern towns and lead to violent clashes.

No Chemistry
Brando and Anna Magnani (in *The Fugitive Kind*) were mismatched onscreen, and in life. He bullied the older star on the set, but eventually agreed to let her share top billing—in Italy.

SIDNEY LUMET

Only a couple of months younger than Brando, Sidney Lumet was a child actor who served in the Far East during the Second World War, and then worked to become a television director. It was that training that earned him his first low-budget feature (and a tremendous critical success) with *12 Angry Men*. He and Brando clearly worked well together on their only collaboration, *The Fugitive Kind*, so it's a pity that

Brando and Lumet (on the *Fugitive* set) got along once the director passed Brando's rigorous round of "mind games."

they have never combined since. Lumet's career (though up and down) has led to such notable pictures as *Long Day's Journey Into Night*, *The Pawnbroker*, *Serpico*, *Dog Day Afternoon*, *Network* and *The Verdict*—exactly the kind of film that might have suited Brando (though it's unlikely anyone could have bettered Paul Newman).

Island Paradise

A publicity picture taken during the shooting of *Mutiny on the Bounty* shows the ripening feeling between Mr. Christian (Brando) and the Tahitian discovery, Tarita.

The director, Sidney Lumet, will tell a fascinating story about a long speech Brando's character has. He has trouble with it, forgetting his lines. They go past take five, more than Lumet has ever had to do with Brando. The director realizes that the key line the actor keeps missing is relevant to his own private life. He thinks of intervening. But Brando insists on carrying on. After two-and-a-half hours, they get it right on take 34. Afterward, Lumet consoles him and there is the kind of exchange that bespeaks magic still: 'I told him that I might have been able to help him but felt it wasn't my right. He looked at me and smiled as only Brando can smile, so that you think daybreak has come. 'I'm glad you didn't,' he said. We hugged and went home."

Such moments are all the more precious in the light of what follows: *Mutiny on the Bounty*, a clear-cut disaster, the first that is laid at Brando's feet but an event that has a large influence on the rest of his life.

Fighting Words

The screen animosity between Bligh and Christian was matched by the actors' real-life feuds. "He hasn't a friend in the world," said a disgusted Trevor Howard. "He never speaks to anyone unless it's someone smaller or younger."

In 1959, MGM decides to remake its 1935 classic about Captain Bligh and Fletcher Christian, the one with Charles Laughton and Clark Gable. Brando is not keen at first, but he is led to reconsider by two things: his mounting financial need and his realization that the mutineers became some of the first Westerners at large in the Pacific. He urges that the picture carry on beyond the mutiny to cover those events. And in that bargaining he gains absolute script approval in return for $500,000 plus ten percent of the gross, $10,000 a week in expenses and an additional $5,000 for every day the picture goes over schedule.

These are extraordinary terms because Brando is not just handsomely paid for his work. He will also receive ten cents of every dollar paid to see the film (the gross—not the net, which is the income minus all the expenses put into a film by actual production or inspired accounting techniques). It might be noted that if an actor has script approval as well as a penalty payment for every extra day, then he is under no pressure to compromise. Without quite understanding its own largesse, MGM has declared that this picture will be so big it will cost whatever it costs.

Who knows if it is the best decision, but Brando will play Fletcher Christian—which ensures that the story gets to the Pitcairn Islands, even if Bligh may be the more tempting role. In the event, Bligh will be played by Trevor Howard. The crew is largely British: Richard Harris, Hugh Griffith, Gordon Jackson. And the picture is in the hands of veteran novelist and screenwriter Eric Ambler, and director Carol Reed (*Odd Man Out*, *The Fallen Angel*, *The Third Man*).

It sounds marvelous. They will shoot in Tahiti itself; there will be a reproduction of the *Bounty*, costing half a million; the best of drama and history will be fused. But Ambler and Reed are a little late in learning that Brando has script approval. And Ambler begins on a process of delivering pages and entire versions only to learn that Brando is not pleased with them. Not that the actor can always say why clearly enough for his notes to be useful.

Ambler is still writing as the cast and crew depart for the Pacific in November 1960. And Brando is still saying "I'm not getting to you. You don't understand." Ambler is being paid $3,000 a week—a lot for a writer—so he is not quickly put off. But he reaches a point where he tells Carol Reed that he doesn't think Brando wants to finish the picture. So Ambler resigns, and is replaced by Charles Lederer.

Filming is already under way. Brando beholds the native women of Tahiti and he falls in love with Tarita Teriipaia. He develops a fondness for the islanders and determines to live in Tahiti. He believes that he has found paradise. Brando spends more time with the women. The script continues to go through changes. And somehow, Brando—a failed director on his own project—is taking over this epic production. One day Reed gives Brando notes on direction and the actor answers that he doesn't see it that way. There is a standoff and Reed resigns from the picture.

Soon thereafter, Brando will profess his horror. He says that he has liked and admired Reed and that MGM has actually fired its own director. He will sue the *Saturday Evening Post* when it alleges that Brando has been chiefly responsible for the delays and inflation on the picture. Few in Hollywood doubt the charge. Brando's eventual performance in the film—as a foppish English naval officer—is exquisite and fascinating. It is a daring impersonation, yet reviews are harsh. But to get there he has alienated every other actor on the film, Carol Reed and his replacement, Lewis Milestone. Actor Richard Harris calls Brando "a large dreadful nightmare," and the studio reckons that the picture has added at least $6 million in costs because of the delays. Its final budget is $30 million, and its total income is less than half that sum. Even so, if it grosses $10 million, Brando will get $1 million from that.

In those early '60s, Hollywood puts together a string of massive failures: *Cleopatra, Dr. Dolittle, 55 Days at Peking, The Fall of the Roman Empire*. The flops lead to changes that put more weight on those few actors who can command a large following at the box office and thus earn a percentage of the proceeds. But Brando's personal reputation suffers, and here are three flops in a row: *One-Eyed Jacks, The Fugitive Kind, Mutiny on the Bounty*—as proof of the man's increasing vanity and egomania. The long crisis that began around *On the Waterfront* has peaked, and the world's most audacious actor is looked upon as mercenary, self-regarding and overweight.

Tender Moment
Brando's affinity for the native Tahitians is obvious in this off-guard moment with an island small-fry.

Decline
1961–1970

"THE GREATEST ACTOR"

I have been at pains in describing this life to remind you how little reason there is to trust actors—or to see actors as the accumulated wisdom (or superiority) of their parts. All too often, actors don't know what they are saying, or why they are doing something. They may not have read the whole script; or they may be laboring on a project where there is no finished script, with no way of judging what this thing is "about." So it is "about" a million dollars or ten days more before the wrap. Actors get cynical, resigned; and we should know enough to have the same way out. But the dynamic of the movies is to make us imagine they are like us, that they know it and feel it, and can be trusted with the resemblance. So, whether the actor is John Wayne, Cary Grant or Marlon Brando, people grow up "identifying."

What does that identification mean? It is as if we prized it so much that we still hardly know how to examine the transaction. So few people have the heart or the head to map out their own fantasy involvement with these phantoms. Yet we have begun to discern that when we vote for someone—when we ask ourselves, do we "like" them, and might they be "like" us—so we are resorting to games or strategies acquired at the movies. Similar things happen when we fall in love, or out of it. I cannot prove that; I would not know how to try. And I respect that aspect of our times that prefers to have large ideas proved. But that does not stop my feeling that love and democracy (both of which

Comrades
Jane Fonda (with Brando on the set of *The Chase*) was in awe of her costar, and not just for his acting. The young starlet was also inspired by his militant activism; soon she would visit Hanoi.

ought to be important) are matters where we have been trained in the movie dark by something that is generally called "stardom."

So "Marlon Brando" is not simply a matter of movie criticism or celebrity gossip (though both of those genres are at work; it's not just the weight of dollars and the bulk of Brando—though those are important, too). It's a matter of hope. And how far that hope has sucked the life out of Brando himself.

We are at the start of what are the most depressing years, the era in which the world lost its faith in Brando—and I have tried to indicate how far, more than any other American actor, he had exerted that pull on us. Consider the responsibility. There is a moment in these years ahead on *The Chase* (1966)—maybe the only halfway decent film from the period—when Brando is doing a scene with Jane Fonda. She is his junior by thirteen years. She is a very serious young actress, and a good one. More than that, she is Henry Fonda's daughter, so she will have heard the story of Brando growing up, just as she has seen most of his great films. She admires him—I am not suggesting or hinting that they had an affair—and loves him as an actor. She thinks she knows how good he is. And she has observed the decline, the dismay.

Well, in this scene from *The Chase*, with Arthur Penn directing, they have worked over their lines and what to do. They have it "down," as they say. Then Brando comes up with something new—it doesn't really matter what it is—a move, a new line, a look. He creates it. It comes up out of him in response to the work. And it is dazzling. With absolute candor she looks at him and says something like "You really are the greatest actor."

And he is still, or could be—if a moment lasted a decade. And by 1966 (he is only forty-two) think how many young men, actors, have come up to him—"but don't let me interrupt your dinner, please"—and said something like Fonda did, and what he means to them, to say nothing of how many young women have let him have them in the fullest way they can think of, as if they long to be touched or infected. Then think of Marlon Brando as the man who will look back on this time and write, "I think of my middle age as the Fuck You Years." This is not to put the responsibility for indifference on anyone but Marlon Brando. But think of the load, think how far his terrible eating is a response to all those interrupted dinners, and remember the great roar and scream he is uttering when we first see him in *Last Tango in Paris*. I want you to feel the horror that besets such a man as he fails.

Here's another anecdote from these bad years. It is 1968. Carlo Fiore comes to have dinner with Brando, an old friend who has not seen too much of him in recent years. They have drifted apart after Brando fired Fiore from *One Eyed Jacks* (where he still got a credit as associate producer). Brando is wearing a poncho on a hot evening. Carlo urges him to take it off.

"Why should I take it off?"

"Because I can't see your body, and so I can't tell what shape you're in."

So Brando obliges him and Fiore sees the fat and the flab. He eats a quart of ice cream, a couple of chickens at a sitting. "I'm not fat by nature," he writes in his autobiography. "I got fat mostly because I loved brownies, ice cream and everything else that makes you fat. One reason for this, I suspect, is that when I was a kid, I'd come home from school to find my mother gone and the dishes in the sink. I'd feel low and open the icebox, and there would be an apple pie, along with some cheese, and the pie would say: 'C'mon, Marlon, take me out. I'm freezing in here. Be a pal and take me out, and bring out Charlie Cheese, too.' Then I'd feel less lonely."

Self-pity? Childish? Yes, of course, and evidence of all those hours mis-spent with doting analysts that would have been better spent with a nutritionist. To say nothing of finding the curiosity to ask, well, if mother was always gone, how was that pie in the icebox? Brando has been in the practice, when still young, of going into hard training before a film, and dropping thirty or forty pounds. But he is too fleshy, too waxy, already in *The Wild One*, in *On the Waterfront*, in *Guys and Dolls*.

Well, why not? He's American, isn't he, a country boy who never had too much schooling—and just because he's brilliant, don't conclude that he's what you might call smart or intelligent. He's also lonesome, well-off, depressive, disappointed—this is America, where sometime in their forties so many people get the notion that the pursuit of happiness is a fraud. Think of Orson Welles—a midwesterner too, who lost his mother when he was nine, an orphan by sixteen, brilliant, and far smarter than Brando. And somehow when he had *Citizen Kane* on one arm and Rita Hayworth on the other, he ate himself to a size where he could not always get out of a limousine. The horror.

These are also years in which Brando fights terrible court battles with Anna Kashfi for custody of their son, Christian. She turns violent, epileptic,

Out of Control

In this famous 1961 photo, Anna Kashfi slaps Brando during a court session about visitation rights to Christian.

unstable—it is easy to say she is not a fit mother. But Brando has other children, other liaisons. He will admit to a time of his life where he goes after other men's wives out of hostility and vengeance—but vengeance for what? For the loneliness, the ice cream. He will admit to so many women that he sometimes cannot remember names and faces. At the same time, with Tarita—a beautiful, serene Tahitian woman—there may be real comfort, rapport, a true relationship. And yet he sees Christian becoming increasingly fearful, alienated, orphanlike.

He buys islands in Tahiti. He spends time there. He tries to develop the local economy. He finds tranquillity and wisdom in the Tahitian philosophy—the very things he claims he needs most in life. But he is also driven by money—the households to support, the children to pay for—and he makes wretched deals in his time of need. And then deals that are vicious and ugly as if to make up for earlier stupidity.

Two Kings

Brando and Yul Brynner (above in a scene from *Morituri*) didn't get along—a now-familiar pattern. At first, Brando wanted to play his part bald—and make Brynner wear a wig.

He is a mess, and so is his nation, of course. And, just like a child, he is moved by every disaster—by Vietnam, by the pathos and anger of blacks, by Native Americans—and he tries to be part of those movements just as the young actor always became the people he was with. But sooner or later all of those angry, urgent moods look at him and say, you're just a fat, sex-happy celebrity and your time has gone. Actors need to be writers or authors of their own art, to be able to put some of this down in a form that will move others. But actors wait for scripts, for projects, for their "right" people and Brando is forty, overweight, with a string of failures and the earned reputation for being too difficult on a picture.

You can see how some people, bolder, firmer, more rational, more purposeful, might have gone away, to Tahiti, or further, all the way up the river, like Colonel Kurtz in *Apocalypse Now*. But Marlon Brando stays, on Mulholland Drive, in a house built for Howard Hughes. Doesn't he remember that Hughes, too, went thoroughly and crazily away?

Outspoken American

To promote *The Ugly American*, Brando (right, in a scene from the film) went on an unprecedented world tour. His fiery condemnation of racism caused many southern theaters to boycott the film. But the movie itself was tame.

GETTING UGLY

One can write off the Brando of the mid-'60s easily enough, by showing that all the films were failures commercially, and misguided ventures: *The Ugly*

American (1963); *Bedtime Story* (1964); *Morituri* (1965); *The Chase* (1966); *The Appaloosa* (1966); *A Countess from Hong Kong* (1967). In the ordinary range of video stores, those films are hard to find nowadays. There's no doubt that they served as a consistent example of decline in the public's mind, and are enough to make the uneasy actor all the more wary of doing anything. Moreover, these strange films coincide with a period of upheaval in America and in the popular awareness of film, inasmuch as the French New Wave films were than breaking on American shores. Of course, that's too simplistic a summary: in 1966, *The Chase* was the boldest attempt made in America to do a film about contemporary society. Whereas, a year later, the same director, Arthur Penn, made *Bonnie and Clyde*—that perfect embodiment of the zeitgeist—while Marlon Brando was caught up in *A Countess from Hong Kong*, that bizarre, bereft attempt to make Chaplin live for a new generation and a project that reduced Brando to appalled comments about the cruelty and insanity of Chaplin.

There are moments of wonder and interest in some of these films, but nothing to overcome the larger dismay—the feeling of why bother?—and all too often that cynicism is suffocating and nauseating. Stewart Stern, the screenwriter on *The Ugly American*, and someone close to Brando for many years, will say, "I don't think he really wanted to work. I think he's always had a tremendous conflict about that anyway. He has enormous regard for people who do useful things in the world. He thinks in some part of his soul that acting is silly. He has a kind of contempt for it." And Brando comes close to agreeing: "If I hadn't been an actor, I've often thought I'd have become a con man and wound up in jail."

With his own company, Pennebaker, on and off in the late '50s, Brando has thought about a movie that deals with the United Nations in the Third World. He wants it to be a picture that shows the altruism and integrity of many field workers, as well as the fatal, and often racist assumptions, of superiority in leaders—on all sides.

This is a very complex subject for an American movie, but Brando has heartfelt notions about the way Americans misperceive the rest of the world. In that sense, Vietnam comes as no surprise to him.

In the '50s, Pennebaker has Stewart Stern write a script on this theme called *Tiger on a Kite*, but it is abandoned. Then a few years later, Pennebaker buys the novel *The Ugly American*, by Eugene Burdick and William J. Lederer, and starts again. It is the story of an American ambassador in a fictional Far East country called Sarkhan.

Pennebaker has floundered as an organization, and in 1962 Brando sells the company to Universal.

In return he receives $1 million, some MCA stock, a pension for his father (who is blamed for a lot of Pennebaker's malaise), and he agrees to do five films for Universal at $270,000 each—a marked reduction on his pay scale from *The Fugitive Kind* and *Mutiny on the Bounty*. *The Ugly American* is the first of those five films, with Brando's old friend, the inexperienced George Englund, directing.

The film does not work; it is talky and dull, not dangerous, penetrating or shocking. Yet Brando's own performance as an initially snooty man, an Ivy League know-it-all who grows into doubt and dismay, is still worth studying. If only, one thinks, this had been *The Quiet American* (that terse Graham Greene novel about early American bungling in Indochina), with Brando as Pyle (the naïve American troublemaker), Trevor Howard as Fowler, the sour English journalist, and Carol Reed directing.

The gap between hit and miss in the movies is so small: *The Quiet American* is filmed in the late '50s, with Joseph Mankiewicz directing, Audie Murphy as Pyle and Michael Redgrave as Fowler. It is a disaster—no one gets the political point (when maybe there was time still to learn from it). And a few years later, there was Brando working with Trevor Howard and Carol Reed , on another project—another disaster. But not even God and Hollywood gets these arrangements straight—so how can a mere actor be held responsible?

So he lurches into *Bedtime Story*, a comedy, and Brando himself is heard to admit, alas, he can't do comedy. It is another Universal chore, with Ralph Levy directing, and David Niven and Shirley Jones as co-stars. It's not just that it ends up unamusing and uninteresting—it is maybe the first Brando film for which the decision to go ahead is inexplicable.

Bedtime for Brando

In the 1964 comedy *Bedtime Story*, Brando and Niven play lovable con men. "God, Niven made me laugh so hard," Brando said later. The film was remade in 1988 (with Steve Martin and Michael Caine) as *Dirty Rotten Scoundrels*.

Then Twentieth Century-Fox comes back into Brando's life with that outstanding picture commitment they hold on him. So he agrees to make *Morituri*, and nothing is more dreadful or depressing to onlookers. It is a World War II story about a German outsider (Robert Crain) who is living in India. He hates the war and is anti-Nazi, so he yields to British intelligence (in the form of Trevor Howard) and agrees to pretend to be SS on a German cargo ship, diverting its valuable rubber cargo to the Allies. Yul Brynner is captain of the ship and Janet Margolin is the one woman on board, Jewish, under threat from everyone.

The script is being written by Daniel Taradash (who won an Oscar adapting *From Here to Eternity*), and one day he gets a phone call from Akim Tamiroff urging him to do his best, because this project is so promising. Of course, it is Brando doing Akim Tamiroff. In time, Brando gets Aaron Rosenberg as producer and Bernhard Wicki, a German, as director, and then begins to humiliate them.

To this day, *Morituri* is held up in Hollywood as a project that helped ruin the old business. There are story conferences of a kind, reported by Taradash: "Brando would . . . curl up in a chair in the corner in a fetal position. He was the Method actor carried to the wildest extreme. And he had complete control! He would like a scene one day. Next day he would say, 'I can't do this. Let's do it this way.' I would say, 'You're not doing this. It's the character.'"

With Wally Cox helping him, Brando starts to re-write the script. Soon thereafter he bars Wicki from his own set. The pace of shooting slows beyond all reason. Yul Brynner determines to stay above the chaos. Observers note Brando—in character—wandering around the set, waiting to think of something to say. At one point he stares out of a porthole on the set— because he has his lines written up on a blackboard on the other side. There is a peculiarly odious atmosphere built up around the very nervous Janet Margolin—as if Brando feels compelled to add to the menace her character feels.

The script and the story may be poor. Wicki, with little English, may be out of his depth. But few witnesses doubt how Marlon Brando is the source of the madness on the picture—an actor in total control, but with no idea where to go. It is a shaming experience and a wretched result. Pauline Kael will say of it, "Like many another great actor who has become fortune's

WALLY COX

Brando urged his troubled friend Cox (wide awake in 1953) to join Alcoholics Anonymous, but he refused.

Wally Cox (1924–73), was a friend of Brando's from school. As a comic television actor (*Mr. Peepers*, *Hiram Holliday*), Cox played mild characters, as befit his slight physical appearance. (He later became a regular on *Hollywood Squares*.) But in life, Cox was far more outgoing, a womanizer and a natural companion on many of Brando's adventures. Cox made a few movies, too, yet he and Brando never actually worked together. Still, Cox was often to be seen on Brando's sets, advising the great man, or just hanging out. When Cox died of a coronary, an empty pill bottle was found nearby, and there were rumors of suicide. He and Brando had drifted apart for a few years, but Brando came back from Tahiti for the service, saying that he alone understood Cox. He put Cox's photograph next to that of his own mother and said, "He was my brother . . . I talk to him all the time."

fool, he plays the great ham . . . as pleased with the lines as if he'd just thought them up."

The Chase is something very different. Brando is prevailed upon to act in it by Sam Spiegel (the producer of *On the Waterfront*), who thinks that in taking a Horton Foote novel and having a screenplay by Lillian Hellman, with Arthur Penn directing, he has a prestigious critique of American society. Brando is to play the sheriff in a Texas town controlled by the local oil tycoon (E. G. Marshall). The action is prompted when a young man (Robert Redford) escapes from the local penitentiary. Inadvertently, he comes back to the town where his wife (Jane Fonda) is now having an affair with the tycoon's son (James Fox). This melodrama is offset by a very rancid portrait of the townspeople—depraved, sex-mad, violent, bigoted, looking for trouble.

No Stereotypes
Brando (in *The Appaloosa*) refused to kill Indians in any film. And he made *Appaloosa*'s screenwriter read forty books about Native Americans.

And the film ends with the sheriff taking the Redford character into custody, but having him murdered by townspeople, in circumstances that remind every viewer of the way Lee Harvey Oswald was shot (two years earlier) in a Texas police station by Jack Ruby.

The Chase will prove a large box-office failure, unkindly reviewed in America. There is a legend of recrimination hanging over it, in that Spiegel took the project away from Penn at the editing stage and sought to increase the levels of sex and violence. No matter, it seems to me a harrowing undercutting of many American legends (the small town, the sheriff, the essential decency of people) that testifies to the dismay of the 1960s. That it is overdone and over-schematic are legitimate complaints. Still, it is a film filled with passion, and Brando seems confident enough of all the surrounding talent (the cast also includes Robert Duvall, Angie Dickinson, Janice Rule and Jocelyn Brando) to deliver a calm, controlled performance. His sheriff is no super-hero, but he's doing his best and is beaten—*The Chase* includes maybe the bloodiest beating-up sequence to which Brando was ever subject (the actor relishes masochistic scenes). He seems involved and he seems to be acting in a work he believes in. After *Morituri*, this is like a return to life.

The Appaloosa is another Universal project, a revenge Western in which Brando plays a man in pursuit of the bandit who has stolen his horse. It is directed by the young Canadian, Sidney J. Furie, briefly regarded as a hot new talent. He and Brando have vigorous disagreements and Brando defies every insistence that he lose weight, remember his lines and address the project with conviction. The results are predictably bad, and the project never has a chance of being more than routine. But why should acting be a job without its element of routine? Again, people watching say that Brando's evident self-loathing is at the root of the disaffection. Quite literally, he does not want to be doing this. Already by then he has the chance of living in Tahiti, but he has the endless battle for Christian to deal with, as well as the mounting list of dependents. And, as some attest, there is something in Brando that relishes the horror of his own downfall and will not be parted from it.

On the face of things, who could condemn any actor for wanting to be part of Charlie Chaplin's return to filmmaking? It has been ten years since Chaplin made *A King in New York*, and that film was warning enough. But in 1952, the master had had a great hit with *Limelight*. So the plan to have Chaplin direct Brando and Sophia Loren in *A Countess from Hong Kong* is one for which few people had to think hard. Alas.

As he has done all his life, Chaplin proceeds to tell Brando what to say, where to stand, how to stand, the expression to register, the timing, everything. Brando soon sees that he is required to reproduce Chaplin. And every improvisational muscle in his body is offended. Uneasy at comedy, given no real mask or disguise in the film, Brando is expected to become a finesse clown. The results are absurd. To make matters far worse, Brando develops an intense dislike for Chaplin. He sees an autocrat, a bullying father (Chaplin is especially harsh to his son, Sydney), exactly the kind of authority figure that Marlon Brando has grown up loathing. "A remarkable talent but a monster of a man" says Marlon in righteous indignation, hardly guessing how many have said the same thing about Brando himself in these years.

THE BRUSH-OFF

No one ever said that Elia Kazan was an easy companion; and Marlon Brando is proud to admit his problems with authority. It may be marvel enough that they collaborated so fruitfully on one play, *A Streetcar Named Desire*, and three movies—*Streetcar*, *Viva Zapata!* and *On the Waterfront*. Kazan does not have to believe that he "discovered" Brando, but he can read the claim in so many places,

A Mean Man
Predictably, egos—and acting styles—clashed when Brando met Charlie Chaplin. "He was a mean man, Chaplin," said Brando later. "God, he really made me mad."

• On June 3, 1968, a 28-year-old woman claiming to represent a group called S.C.U.M. (Society for Cutting Up Men) shoots Andy Warhol in the chest and abdomen. The woman, Valerie Solanis, was disgruntled that the artist and filmmaker wouldn't produce one of her scripts.

Brando may think, deep in his own mind, that Kazan (and all the rest of them) were lucky to find him—how else could Kazan have found a lever to shift the original balance of the Tennessee Williams play? And Brando has to remember the alteration from being an unknown to being a Broadway sensation, and knowing how much of that depended on Kazan's noticing him. Of course, it is by now an open question whether he is grateful for that, or half in search of vengeance.

Kazan and Brando have not worked together since *On the Waterfront*. Then, in 1969, as Kazan comes to film his own best-selling novel, *The Arrangement*, he thinks of Brando again.

This is a role based on Kazan himself, so Kazan is now asking Brando to be him. But he is wary: he has seen Brando's recent films and he knows the warning signs: the actor being overweight; his palpable indifference to projects. Those are the screen's record of all the stories about Brando's dismay with himself at being an actor, at the lousy American films, the corruption and the money, the lies and the manipulation.

But Brando may be interested in *The Arrangement*. He flirts with it; he keeps Kazan in suspense. He asks the director to come up and visit at the house. It is April 4, 1968, the day on which Martin Luther King Jr. has been killed. As Kazan arrives, Brando is there outside the house, waiting. He falls on the director in grief for the whole country. "He was so intense and so convincing that I didn't realize," Kazan would write later, "he'd walked me back to my car and opened the door to help me in."

With Kazan in the car, Brando says he can't do the part. Kazan drives away, and for all we know the two men will never speak or see each other again. Kirk Douglas gets the part, and Kazan will say "I found him to be terribly bright, very eager, and genuinely enthusiastic. What a relief that was!"

The essential relationship in Brando's creative life is over: a kind of disgust lingers on both sides. Brando can think Kazan abandoned him; the director can believe he was necessary to the actor.

There is no room for sentiment or gratitude. Even in 1999, when Kazan is to receive an honorary Oscar from the Academy, there is no Brando on the Awards night, no reunion, no admission of how much two very difficult, very tricky and very actorly men had needed each other.

PLAYING POLITICS

Time and again, in the bad years, people on film projects believe that they are not getting all of Marlon Brando, or his best, because of the many causes to which he is devoted. Equally, when he is most active with those causes, he is often depicted—by the victims as well as the suspicious press—as just a wealthy, self-indulgent Hollywood star massaging his troubled soul with "involvement." Yet so many of those causes have been happy to entertain the prospect of a very famous actor—and a man often hailed for his honesty—as their spokesman. In turn, he sees that he is being used for "publicity," one of those things he most loathes about being an actor. So, yet again, he is torn

between the charade of public action and the increasing solitude that might live out of sight, far away, in some primitive paradise.

He is the victim of his own feelings. Though he never has the penetrating, analytical intelligence or the natural readiness to find compromise that amounts to talent in politicians, he is easily moved by misfortune, and made angry if he sees some long-term, malign impulse causing it. A person of his temperament has to be bewildered by the way, in the very same years, politics in America becomes increasingly dominated by performance, acting and putting on a show. So just as Marlon Brando, the real citizen, wants to step aside from his celebrity persona, to speak up on behalf of the afflicted and exploited, so he sees a long line of political performers possessed with something he can only regard as devilish cunning as they slip back and forth from reality to illusion. A Ronald Reagan, to Marlon Brando, was a hack actor and a politician who does not bother to care—but Reagan makes just the magical move that torments Brando: he steps out of one fake light and into another, and seems able to call them both sunshine. In comparison, Brando is nearly childlike in his sincerity. And he is appalled, reduced to horror, to see that sincerity counts for so little.

It may never occur to him, and he is not blessed with the irony that could live with the insight, but it is very likely that his greatest political message to America is in Vito Corleone—a man who, along with his son,

On Their Side
Brando addresses a rally of Native Americans in Washington's Malcolm X Park. The Indians walked across the country to protest discrimination. From the looks of his waistline, Marlon took the plane.

Michael, becomes accepted in the last decades of the twentieth century as a model of a necessary, Machiavellian political harshness and pragmatism. The horror.

He has tried. In the late '60s, with his own 16mm camera, in India, he has filmed scenes of absolute poverty. "On my last day of filming, after photographing a child who had died right in front of me, I put my camera down and cried. I couldn't take any more." He shows the footage in Hollywood, and people are moved. One hostess tells him, "We should look after our own." But Jack Valenti, president of the Motion Picture Association of America, says he will take it to President Lyndon Johnson. Perhaps he does—no word comes back. Brando shows it to the television networks and they say, thank you, but they have their own footage.

He feels initial sympathy for the Black Panthers. In part, as research for *Burn!*, he goes to Oakland in 1968 to meet Bobby Seale and Eldridge Cleaver. They stay up all night talking, and Brando asks Cleaver to read the script for *Burn!* and make comments. But Cleaver doesn't yield to the flattery—he's too tough and too cool to sit down and read a screenplay! Brando stays in touch. He attends court appearances; he gives sums of money to the movement; he attends the funeral of Bobby Hutton and says that Hutton could be his own son. He goes on TV and says that the Oakland police murdered Hutton. It is naïve, and it is seldom separate from Brando's attraction to beautiful black women (which some Panthers may see as the old game of exploitation), but Brando is touched by the weird harmony between this black rejection of American society and the attitude of Johnny in *The Wild One*—"What are you rebelling against?" "Whaddya got?"

There is a far longer, far more reasoned support of Native American causes. He is well read on this subject. He has scholarly support for his claim that in the interests of United States Manifest Destiny, between seven and eighteen million Indians were wiped out. He spends time with various tribes and says how much he likes the plain, shared existence, the lack of pomp, the sardonic humor, the resilience, the story-telling. He becomes close to such leaders as Clyde Warrior, Vine Deloria Jr., Dennis Banks and Russell Means. He appears at fish-ins, at attempts at land occupation and at ordinary marches and demonstrations. He gives money, he speaks to politicians, he does all that he can think of.

Nothing is better remembered than the events of the evening of March 27, 1973. It is Oscar night, and Brando is up for best actor in *The Godfather*. Brando is not at the event himself—he is up on Mulholland Drive, watching it on television. Shortly before the acting award is to be announced, Brando's secretary, Alice Marchak, arrives, with Brando's tickets and a guest—Sacheen Littlefeather, a dark, pretty, twenty-six-year-old with braided hair and a buckskin dress. She has a long speech, written by Brando, which she tells the organizers she will read if Brando wins. They say there will not be time, but they decide not to block her appearance.

Liv Ullmann and Roger Moore announce that Brando is the winner and Sacheen steps forward. She says that Brando "very regretfully cannot accept this very generous award. And the reasons for this are the treatment of the American Indians today by the film industry and in television reruns." She says she has a speech which she will release to the press. There is the suggestion that she is "inauthentic" and that the Oscars incident has been a "stunt." Perhaps it is also a scene created by a rather naïve director. Perhaps Brando's own presence at the Oscars, and his own reasoned rejection of the prize, with a simple reference to Hollywood abuse of Indians and to the current situation, would have been better judged.

Sacheen Littlefeather sounds a little fake, though all research can really dig up is a life story typical of Indians who have had great difficulty adjusting to American society. The American Indian Movement is galvanized by the incident. It is still remembered all over the world. It is a moment when Marlon Brando used public relations pretty effectively.

Yet maybe the most intriguing cause is the one least known, that of Tahiti. It was during the filming of *Mutiny on the Bounty* that Brando was first drawn to the amiable ease of Tahitian life and to beauties like Tarita. At the same time, one day he climbs a mountaintop and sees the far-away island of Teti'aroa. He becomes intrigued and he hires a fisherman to take him to the island. In fact, it is several isles—a coral atoll, with a dozen spots of land, the largest including a beautiful lagoon.

Teti'aroa is owned by an elderly blind woman, Madame Duran, and in 1966–7, in two deals, she sells

INDIAN MAIDEN

Littlefeather at the Oscars, displaying Brando's Indian statement.

She was referred to, variously, as Sacheen or Sasheen Littlefeather—the Indian maiden sent by Marlon Brando to decline his Oscar for *The Godfather*. She was twenty-six and half-Apache, half-Yaqui; she had been born, very poor, on a reservation outside Tucson. Her real name was Maria Louise Cruz, and she was a sometime actress as well as winner of the Miss American Vampire contest for 1970. She had been part of the Native American occupation of Alcatraz, and she was a well-known figure in San Francisco, where she had been public-service director on a rock station. Brando had been in touch with her for several months in his diligent research into Indian attitudes (and pretty women). He inspected and refined her make-up and her very pretty Indian costume before she appeared for her few minutes of celebrity

Brando the islands for $270,000. There is some local resistance to this. In the Tahitian Territorial Assembly, Jacques-Denis Drollet argues that the islands are actually the property of the royal family. But Brando's friend Christian Marquand exerts influence on the French government (Tahiti is also French Polynesia) to have Brando's purchase approved.

He goes there often, once for as long as six months. He will say that the happiest times of his life have been passed there, doing very little. That languid acceptance of passing time is something that appeals to him in the Tahitian nature. He has noted how his own pulse rate falls the longer he stays there. What does he do? He reads, he operates his ham radio, he eats and drinks and he likes to be with Tarita, who has abided by his wish to make no more films but look after their children. He waves away the flies. He sighs at the invasive mildew, the rot. Even paradise has its limits. And Kurtz his madness.

Over the years, he has had grander plans: development, water schemes, tourism. He has built what he calls a hotel and an airstrip, as well as the simple bungalows that house his family and friends. But the larger schemes have foundered, in part because whenever he goes away they languish; because the climate of the islands—the heat, the humidity, the wind—tends to undermine buildings; and perhaps because he lacks the stamina or the resolve. Paradise may be a naïve dream, a place where all things are made balmy, sunny and peaceful. Falling asleep. Until real anguish breaks through and grabs hold of the Brando tribe.

Actor's Aerie
Brando's home high in the Hollywood Hills offers stunning views across Los Angeles—on the occasional days when the town isn't shrouded in smog.

NAUGHTY BOY

He is a naughty boy. He likes to empty rooms by silent farting strategies; he is always on the phone as someone else—it may be his best acting of the '60s—certainly the kind closest to humor or merriment; and there are times when he seems to take it as his right, or curse, to have to fondle every woman who passes by. He uses touch as most men use looking. And granted the climate of the late '60s, even if he doesn't exactly know it, he is, in his prim and increasingly portly way, advancing on something like a pornographic movie.

It is in the mid-to-late '60s that the American cinema changes sexually, and at much the same moment the unequivocal stud of an earlier era begins to be bloated, gray, out of breath even. It's not just that he has seemed for a while the most beautiful man in the world—far more, he has made that kind of language safe (as well as seductively dangerous). You couldn't say that about Gary Cooper in 1930 without being prey to suggestions of pansy-ness. But Brando has enough sweat, violence and poetry about him to make the word "beauty" negotiable. Then he loses the beauty and learns what women have always known—that no decline is crueller than the loss of beauty.

Sex is everywhere—on the screen (the American screen), with nakedness, language and the unmistakable sense of what people do; it is live on the stage; it is in advertising and on TV; and it is in the way nearly every woman dresses. But in the movies, he seems to have been passed by a clutch of younger beauties, most of whom know their debt to him but can't help looking younger, hotter, sexier. There is Robert Redford in *Butch Cassidy and the Sundance Kid* (as well as Paul Newman, who now looks ten years fresher than Brando), there is Warren Beatty, Steve McQueen and very soon there will be Nicholson, Pacino, De Niro. And, more or less, they are getting it from babes up there on the screen. While Marlon Brando remembers the days when the rape scene meant a fadeout.

Does it occur to you around 1968 that Marlon Brando has never been anywhere near doing it on screen? It may be clear from the public press how much he does of it in life. And so, in five years, he makes *Reflections in a Golden Eye*, *Candy*, *The Night of the Following Day* and *The Nightcomers*—films in which sex is the subject, the reason for being

Not that *Reflections* is trash or anywhere near it. It is an adaptation of the novel by Carson McCullers, with John Huston as the writer-director. The central male role, Major Weldon Penderton, is a lifetime military man, married, but a repressed homosexual. Indeed, at the climax of the story, this pressure is so great that he will kill a man.

The movie has been talked about for years, but studio money is very nervous—for homosexuality then is not quite admitted to the alleged sexual revolution. Elizabeth Taylor wants to play Penderton's wife, and she tries to set up the picture with her friend Montgomery Clift. But Clift cannot be insured, for reasons soon to be illustrated by his premature death in 1966. It's then that Brando steps in, tempted by the dangerous material, inclined to do it out of respect for Clift, and intrigued by the prospect of Huston. But very nervous. He goes to Ireland to see Huston. Huston watches and respects the actor's great need to get inside a part—to be possessed by it. Brando reads the script, and then takes a long walk in the rain before saying he will do it.

ALWAYS THE HAM

Telephones, ham radios and, in recent years, the Internet give Brando priceless anonymity.

Remember the Brando who always liked gadgets? Well, it turns out, in later years, Brando grew obsessed with the telephone. Over the years, he developed a talent and a taste for calling up people (friends or not) at eccentric hours and pretending to be someone else. The mimicry is extraordinary—like that of Peter Sellers—and Brando loves to startle people by knowing intimate things about them. Of course, the phone is also a hiding place for someone too shy to appear in public. And it leads to Brando's great enthusiasm for ham radio, yarning the nights away talking to strangers on different continents, seldom revealing his true identity. Is this the natural final destination for a chronic actor? Is this his last great freedom?

Rock Bottom

"There's always a bottom for everybody," said Brando's *Candy* costar, James Coburn, "and I had the impression that this was what was happening here." Ewa Aulin is in the background.

As if to match the presence of Taylor and Huston, Warners agrees to pay Brando $1 million again.

Encouraged by Huston, he takes on one of his least glamorous looks—a plain, plump man with hair slicked down: Brando thinks often of what might have happened if the Shattuck cadet had gone all the way. He works hard on the picture and feels encouraged by the room Huston leaves to actors. He does brilliant work—especially in scenes with Julie Harris. He has felt himself all the way into the frozen soul of this effete soldier, and seen no reason to make the man gratuitously appealing. It is an extraordinary example of sheer acting. The film proves to be a major failure. Yet Julie Harris observes her old friend with deep regret: "He was innately brilliant but it was all scattered, almost as if he'd been told early on that he was nothing and worthless. Yet his work was so beautiful and so pure that there was no explaining where it came from. He still didn't love acting, he didn't love the theater and he didn't respect his own talent, but his gift was so great he couldn't defile it."

Still, he tries. *Candy* is a novel by Terry Southern, a reworking of Voltaire's *Candide*, with the young male hero replaced by a nubile but empty-headed blonde. It is proposed as a film with Frank Perry directing and Hayley Mills in the leads, but her father John Mills will not allow this. So Perry drops out, and the direction is offered to Christian Marquand, in part because he says he can get Brando to do a week's work on it. Buck Henry writes the script and Brando is one of an "all-star" male cast, doing a week's work for $50,000, ogling a young Swedish discovery, Ewa Aulin.

Brando plays the Great Guru Grindl in Indian robes, a wig and a caste mark on his forehead. It is foolish nonsense, but as life will have it Brando hits on the very attractive Aulin during the filming. In ordinary circumstances, such a transaction is accomplished easily enough, but Aulin has a kind of hysterical breakdown which takes the form of helpless laughing at Brando on the set. (As so often, fate is given a blind eye: here is a fine subject for a comedy—the aging womanizer, the perfect nymph, and her not being able to stop laughing, his increasingly demented search for some gravity that may calm her.)

The Night of the Following Day is made for little other reason than to satisfy Universal's contract right to five films. A gang kidnaps an heiress, but then one of the gang elects to rescue the victim. The gang consists of Richard

Boone, Brando as the guy who changes sides, and Rita Moreno as a druggie.
It is directed by Hubert Cornfield (son of a Twentieth Century-Fox executive)
and filmed in a wild part of Brittany.

No one (other than Brando) can see the sense in casting Rita Moreno—
not because of her acting, but because it is widely known that she has had an
affair with Brando over many years. She is married now and she brings her
husband and child to the location. Nevertheless, the affair resumes and
carries over into one prolonged, violent sexual scene in which people on set
are amazed to see Brando and Moreno losing their characters and becoming
themselves. The film has no other interest, alas, beyond this bizarre kind of
self-embarrassment. But as others suggest, this is the real state of Brando's
life—one in which he wilfully cuckolds husbands and humiliates women
(by having other women arrive during lovemaking) and for once it has spilled
over onto art's screen. But that is what the '60s liked to think they were
about. And it is mirror image of Brando's contempt for his own acting.

Last of this group is *The Nightcomers*, filmed in England and directed by
Michael Winner. The film is derived from the Henry James novella *The Turn of
the Screw*, and covers the action that leads up to James' story. Brando plays
Peter Quint, and Stephanie Beacham is the governess. The sole novelty of the
film is the intensity of the sexual affair enjoyed by these two characters.
Even for 1971–2, the filming was daring—there is a great deal of Beacham to

Night Fight

In *The Night of the Following Day*,
a low-budget quickie shot in
France, Brando and Rita Moreno
had a real-life fight during a staged
fight scene; much of their brawl
made it into the film.

behold. The actress went along with it all gamely, and reports a very friendly association with Brando, no matter how much he teases her. At one point, he ties her to the bed so securely that she can't get free at the lunch break. It is a film full of sadomasochism, uncomfortable, but seeming to beg for some more complete or challenging exposure. Without plan or advanced knowledge, one can still feel Brando advancing on the full sexual fury and dismay of *Last Tango in Paris*.

SCORCHED

Amid so many pictures that are depressing already in outline and set-up, *Burn!* is something far out of the ordinary. Even if it was naïve perhaps to seek Black Panther advice on its script, *Burn!* is the kind of project that no other leading Hollywood actor would contemplate. It could be a great tragedy about imperialism and race.

Around the middle of the nineteenth century (this is loosely based on fact), Sir William Walker is sent to the Portuguese-controlled Caribbean island of Queimada. The British intention is to expel the Portuguese military and government from the island in order to secure its valuable sugar resources for themselves. Walker makes friends with a black dock worker, José Dolores,

Burned Out
"Movie acting is just dull, boring, childish work," Brando (with Renato Salvatori) told an interviewer on the set of *Burn!* Partly because of Brando's threats to him, director Gillo Pontecorvo started carrying a gun.

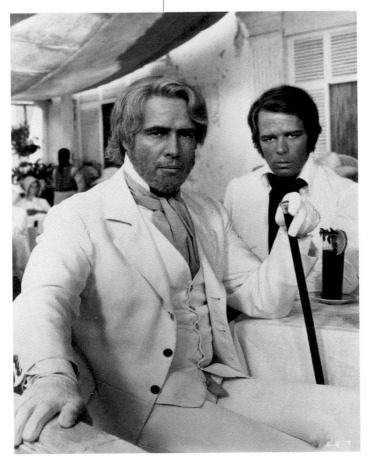

and turns him into the figurehead for insurrection against the Portuguese. The plot works. The Portuguese are thrown out. The British support the new government in return for favored trade terms. José Dolores has been used and betrayed, but the friendship with Walker remains.

Ten years pass. Walker has become cynical and dissolute. But in Queimada, José Dolores is leading a new black revolutionary movement. Walker is hired by the British government to undermine it. He then employs the old Portuguese methods of burning and destroying the terrain in the hunt for rebels. José Dolores is captured and Walker is prepared to let him go free, but José elects to die as a martyr. As he is leaving the island, Walker himself is murdered.

The prospects of a Conradian story are enhanced by the decision to have Gillo Pontecorvo direct the picture. The Italian filmmaker is famous for the pseudo-documentary narrative style of *The Battle of Algiers*, one of the most vivid political pictures ever made. Brando is fascinated by the new project and he signs on with producer Alberto Grimaldi for $750,000. Initial plans are to shoot the film in Colombia.

But in practice, the shooting is a nightmare. The location conditions in Colombia are very bad, and Brando begins to hanker after the comforts he is used to. He develops an ugly rash on his face, and has difficulty getting it treated. There is a great deal of marijuana use among the cast and crew, readily supplied by local sources. There is also constant pilfering of equipment, props and costumes, much of which must then be repurchased in local markets. Brando is also disgusted when he discovers that the production is paying all blacks on the film at a much lower level than the whites.

Moreover, Evaristo Marquez (cast as José Dolores) is a simple cane-cutter who has never acted in his life before. He is very handsome but he cannot keep up with Brando in their scenes together. And far from using the newsreel style from *The Battle of Algiers*, Pontecorvo now feels bound to shoot the film with a static, withdrawn camera. He asks for great detail, meticulously followed, and in the heat and humidity tempers flare as Brando feels the film acquiring a leaden pace.

The arguments turn into open hostility, with Brando even talking of wanting to kill Pontecorvo. So, finally, Brando leaves the location in Colombia with the picture unfinished. Producer Grimaldi threatens to sue him. But the shooting is resumed in Morocco, adding another $750,000 to the bill. When it is done, the film is worthy, but very slow and without any real dramatic interaction among the leading characters. Brando is English again, and quite good in many scenes. He catches the lethargy and fatalism of the aristocrat. But here is a project that needs inspiration and control at the same time—a John Huston, perhaps, or David Lean.

United Artists regards the picture as a disaster and cuts twenty minutes from the Italian version before agreeing to release it in America. The film never finds an audience and comes to be regarded as one more Brando folly. But even in its cut version, there are scenes that show what might have been. Even with a very rich story, a great actor is not enough. So many other elements must come together, and by 1970 Marlon Brando has not had such a happy mixture for years. At every step, he seems compelled to prove the justice of his gloomy fear—that there is no reason to try making films any longer.

It is only when the film is dead and buried that Brando seems to realize what has been lost. He says then that, despite their quarrels, Pontecorvo is one of the best directors he has worked with. It is as if the project has reverted to being a possibility. It is akin to loving Tahiti, so long as he is in Los Angeles, but not really having the stamina for the place when he is there.

Conflicted Star
After Brando lost interest in *Burn!*, he fled the Colombia set and returned to Los Angeles. But later he praised the film as one of his best.

KENT STATE SHOOTINGS

May 4, 1970
• National Guard troops kill four students during a Vietnam War protest at Kent State University in Ohio. The shootings escalate tension between war protesters and the Nixon government.

Comeback
1971–1973

IN THE GARDEN

It's not so much that Marlon Brando seems older and calmer than he has ever been before in *The Godfather*. He is forty-eight when the film opens, playing a man who must be sixty but who actually moves as if he were over seventy. One way Vito Corleone's authority is made gracious and sweet is that he pushes the notional age of the character upward. Has all that respect aged him, or worked like gravity? The actor "ages" very skillfully: he does wonders with his mouth and face—you can wonder even if Vito has had a slight stroke already. And, of course, he has the one tranquil death scene in the film—not the least thing that places him above Mob behavior. But the entire film extends a kind of emeritus status toward Vito and Brando. He does not actually do very much. He sits in his chair. He sits at a meeting or two. He lies in a hospital bed.

He buys a little fruit. And he sits in his last garden. And as if Marlon Brando himself had grown weary of being tired, perplexed, dismayed, troubled, hounded, so the stillness of *The Godfather* is merciful. It lets us see the rare finesse that can own a film while hardly ever having to get up.

Oh, yes, he dances. And it is like God dancing—not merely elegant, but something one never thought to see. So it is the serenity of Vito Corleone that is most gratifying, if you love Brando. The wrecked ship has come home and become a noble antique overnight. Is that fanciful or sentimental? I don't think so.

FRANCIS FORD COPPOLA

Francis Ford Coppola was only 31 when Paramount hired him to direct *The Godfather*. What's more, he had not yet had a real success. *Finian's Rainbow* had flopped and *The Rain People* had done modestly. But Coppola had won much respect for his work on the screenplay for *Patton*. What Paramount hardly knew was how far his family background prepared him for the Corleones. Francis's father had been a flutist with Toscanini and a failed

Coppola (with Brando on the set of *Apocalypse Now*) got his start working on low-budget Roger Corman movies. On his own films, the budgets soared.

composer—a very ambitious but rather embittered man. And Francis had grown up a bit of a weakling, overawed by a flamboyant and brilliant older brother—rather like Fredo with Sonny. (Coppola's brother is the scholar August Coppola, who is Nicolas Cage's father.)

Rather, the casting of Brando here reaches out toward benign wisdom just as much as it seemed to say to the group of young actors around him, yes you have grown up the right way. *The Godfather* is, not least, about a way of acting. And if Marlon Brando, off-set, mooned passers-by, with Jimmy Caan and the others, that's fine and grand—just not quite Vito's style.

How does it happen? Well, it is folklore now—first that many actors are yearning to play this role (from Frank Sinatra to Orson Welles); second that the young Francis Ford Coppola, who is on most uneasy ground with Paramount in doing this picture, thinks of Brando; and third, that Paramount, including its self-adoring production boss, Robert Evans, regards Brando in 1971 as finished, over the hill, a liability. Or worse.

It is also the case that Mario Puzo, author of the book, had thought of Brando first and sent him galleys. So Coppola persists and Paramount puts up a challenge: Brando, but no more than $50,000, with a security bond, and he must take a screen test. Coppola practices guile. He tells Brando that, really, they need to experiment, to see if Marlon can age adequately. So the actor works out a look and Coppola films it on video. He even begins to improvise. And Coppola sees something like a marvel coming to life.

The deal is improved a little: Brando will get $100,000 and ten percent of the profits. He begins to be involved. He backs Coppola in arguing for Al Pacino as Michael (the studio wanted Warren Beatty). Brando seems to see how Michael should be less handsome, more inward. And as the film begins, Brando becomes a stalwart supporter of the young director, but Paramount is still not sure of Coppola. There are stories of another expert director being held in reserve—it may even be Elia Kazan—which might make Brando that much more faithful to Coppola. There is a threat to fire Coppola, and Brando retaliates by saying that if the director goes, he goes too.

The filming occurs in 1971, with several real Mafiosi there to inspect the product. Coppola gains in confidence. But still there are those saying that between them, cinematographer Gordon Willis and set designer Dean Tavoularis have given the film too dark a look. Others say it is very violent. Others still think it may glorify the Mafia. And when he is shown a rough cut, Marlon Brando believes it is no good and that he has done bad work.

How would you trust an actor?

But he backs his judgment. He is, once more, in urgent need of cash and so he renegotiates his contract. For another $100,000 up front, he will sacrifice his points interest. It will be estimated later that he has thereby deprived himself of over $10 million. This should not be left out of account in trying to explain his reluctance to appear on Oscars night. He was bitter as well as righteous—a deadly combination, so far beneath old man Vito Corleone.

Of course, it doesn't matter. Film brings a kindness to the life of actors, one modest thing to offset the many real travails they encounter—in the form of both success and failure. That Marlon Brando by the age of sixty-five has not managed the look of Vito Corleone may sadden him. (In the same way exactly, Orson Welles was many times larger—and far more cheerful—than the old man he played in *Citizen Kane*.) Vito Corleone goes on,

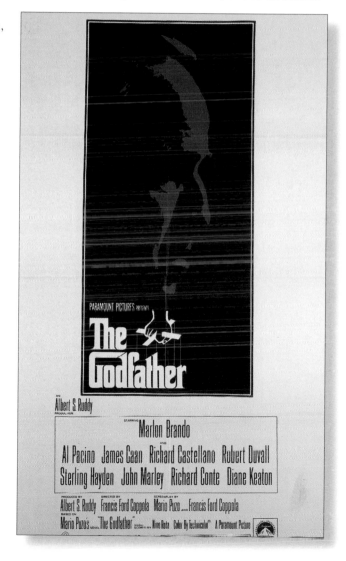

Puppet Master
The sinister poster image on which Paramount sold *The Godfather* suggested it was a film about Vito Corleone, when truly, Michael (Al Pacino) is the central character.

a model father and grandfather, a man who has given his children so much more than he had. A very American hero. Brando says, early on, that he likes the ironic vision in *The Godfather*, but does he mean the way in which wickedness comes to be an ideal?

Does the actor understand the film? He doesn't need to. There's no doubt that the guy who was wearied by his own *One-Eyed Jacks* could never have made anything as lucid or sinister as *The Godfather*. Yet Coppola could not have made it without him. And when Robert De Niro comes to recreate the younger, Sicilian Vito in *The Godfather Part II*, he pays huge, actorly respect to Brando's face and speech. Above all, though, he knew in advance the benign gaze of the country boy, a man who could see through all violence and damage and feel the ripeness of tomatoes in his last garden.

It comes to this, I think—Brando has done several great things, several that changed the arts and acting. But in Vito Corleone, he gives us his best American, and an idyllic portrait of how an accomplished man might grow older and die perfectly.

THE CAT

Remember that gray cat? Gray with a white belly, and a dab of white on the nose. It is a lean cat, a working cat. Why not? This is a cat prowling around the set, a place where there may be many mice and a few cocky rats. This is not a cat that was in the script so that the production design was charged to find a cat—a sweet obedient creature with a cat wrangler in case it had actorly moods. No, this is an impromptu cat, unforeseen, unintended, until Marlon Brando on what he knows will be his first scene in the picture, having satisfied himself about the tailored fit of his tuxedo and the perfection of the red rose in his button-hole, having his lines in his head, having prepared to the best of his ability, still, walking to the set, happens to see the gray cat, bends down and scoops it up, so that the cat is in his lap in that first scene.

The writer, Mario Puzo, has not put it there; neither the director, Francis Coppola nor the design chief, Dean Tavoularis. But no one watching fails to be moved by the genius and the spontaneity of the actor's decision. It is not just that the detail is "right" or lovely or beautiful; it is that Brando has become Vito Corleone—that he has the confidence, the authority, of the man, the onetime Sicilian peasant, the country boy, the animal lover. And Brando takes the chance that he might be scratched by an angry cat. It might be

Purr Genius
Brando's portrayal of Don Corleone seems effortless, despite his inability to remember lines, which were often scrawled on his hands or shirt cuffs.

feral, dangerous. But the cat feels the hands of power. It rolls over on its back and lets Brando's large white hand rest on its warm belly. Cats belong to no one, but they will hire out for a moment—like whores. And this cat feels relaxed. Brando, too, must feel some ease, and he has made a great gift to the picture by letting us see the simplicity of Vito Corleone, the boyish pleasures he enjoys, the sensuality of the feeling for fur. See what an actor can do for a picture! See how an actor can make you fall in love with a man, or a character—whatever Vito Corleone is, out there, on the edge of reality.

Then as the scene goes on, and Vito has other supplicants, he puts the cat on his desk and the cat is never seen again. And then the film takes over. There is a scene outside in the garden, at the wedding party, with Michael and Kay: he is in Marine uniform still; she has that red dress with white polka dots and a straw hat. She sees Luca Brasi getting ready to have an audience with Vito, and Michael tells her the story of how, long ago, to persuade the bandleader who had Johnny Fontane's contract, his father and Luca Brasi visited the bandleader and made him the offer he couldn't refuse: his signature or his brains on the release contract. "That's a true story," Michael tells her, and she doesn't knows how to take it. "It's my family, Kay," Michael adds, "not me."

Rear-Guard Action
During filming of *The Godfather*'s outdoor wedding scene, Brando (with Talia Shire) dropped his pants and mooned the entire cast, including children.

It is also something else—a true story—we know about Vito, the cat lover. Something stark, brutal, cold—yet actually not quite as cold as Al Pacino's Michael, who tells the contract story in a way that we can't quite tell whether he is possessed by horror or disdain for his own family. Or pride. In the film, therefore, we have learned something profound and dismaying about this old peasant father who looks so grand in a tuxedo. And we have met a force as great as Brando's: Al Pacino. *The Godfather* is, among many other things, a study in how to act, or how to offer generosity, hope and warmth in acting—or not. This is something over which a Brando, or any actor, has no control. It is the work, the movie, the drama and the directing.

And Brando's beguiling presence, so palpably dangerous yet so human, so able to order up retribution, yet moving gingerly as he goes to dance, having to turn on the feeble Johnny Fontane, slap him, growl at him like a toy lion, the godfather who pulls the flimsy singer together, shows him out of the door and then turns with one of Brando's best, dismissive sighs—as if people to whom he is helplessly attached could be so unworthy (and we half know already that the "good" son, Michael would never feel such an attachment—and does not really love Kay, never has, never will), we know that this potent godfather is the father of sons he might wish more or less for.

The brilliant shape of the film has let us see them already: the outcast, Michael; the semi-invalid, Fredo; the reckless, thoughtless Sonny. No wonder this Vito has an extra "son," the adopted Tom—for none of his sons is "right." And his power can do nothing about it except grieve. Vito Corleone is a man set in sadness, the common regret of a onetime Sicilian kid. A boy who loves cats and so on. And surely admired horses, even the horse about to end up cut in two, with one half bleeding in Jack Woltz's bed, the other already being cut up for meat somewhere.

PARIS MATCH

There is not much sex in *The Godfather*. Sonny humps a bridesmaid behind a closed door; in Sicily, Michael is in awe of the superb breasts of his new wife, Apollonia. But in a uniquely American tradition, the essential sexual urge of humans has been largely subsumed in power and violence. Men who run the world have little need of such things. But *Last Tango in Paris* is about a man who has lost so much—his country, his wife, his character, his dignity. All those acts have been stripped away so that he might be naked beneath his brown cashmere coat. In a modern arena, it's like going from Lear to the Fool in the same moment.

In 1971, Bernardo Bertolucci is thirty-one. He has just had a great success with *The Conformist*. But he has been undergoing psychoanalysis and feels driven to make a film about sexuality—or male sexuality, or his own. He feels that Brando may be uniquely experienced to play the central role. The two men meet in Paris in the spring of 1971, with Brando speaking Tahitian French. He watches *The Conformist* and admires it. Bertolucci outlines the scheme of a film about Paul, this wrecked American in Paris, his wife a suicide.

Death Wish

Don Corleone's death scene in the garden was shot on Brando's last day of work on *The Godfather*. "Give me the negative so I can burn it," he said to cinematographer Gordon Willis as he left. The boy was played by Anthony Gounaris.

BAGGAGE CHECKS

Hoping to counter the hijacking of commercial jets to Cuba, U.S. airlines decide to begin checking baggage for the first time in the summer of 1972.

You will never see the most highly acclaimed film of our time on television.

This may be your last chance to see it in a theatre.

An ALBERTO GRIMALDI Production

Marlon Brando

Last Tango in Paris

with MARIA SCHNEIDER · Maria Michi · Giovanna Galletti · and with JEAN-PIERRE LEAUD
also starring MASSIMO GIROTTI · Produced by ALBERTO GRIMALDI · Directed by BERNARDO BERTOLUCCI
A Film by BERNARDO BERTOLUCCI
A COPRODUCTION PEA PRODUZIONI EUROPEE ASSOCIATE S.A.S-ROME LES PRODUCTIONS ARTISTES ASSOCIES S A–PARIS   United Artists
X NO ONE UNDER 17 ADMITTED

Not Ready for Primetime

The poster for *Last Tango* played up the film's hot sex—for once, not much of an exaggeration. It was Brando's last role as a romantic lead.

Paul meets a young woman and they have a brief, intense physical affair. It will end badly, with the man destroyed. The director adds that he foresees an unusual complicity between himself and Brando, an intense exploration of the issues of sexuality, with a lot of improvisation on the set. Brando is not just intrigued. It is as if, finally, he has found the opportunity for the kind of unbridled delving into his own deepest passion, done in such a way that the actor is not just servant to the concept but one of its authors. And as they talk more, and Brando reveals the great problem he had with his parents, with his dignity (and with women), Bertolucci begins to see that Paul must be Marlon, that improvisation may bring this actor's mystery to the surface. In the event, there are long passages where Paul has Brando's history, his confusion and his strange mixture of violence and lethargy

They meet again in the summer, when Bertolucci has a screenplay. The partnership develops and Bertolucci will say "I had at my disposal a great actor, with all the technical experience any director would require. But I also had a mysterious man waiting to be discovered in all the richness of his personal material."

A deal is done—with producer Alberto Grimaldi, who is still suing Brando over *Burn!* That matter will be dropped. Bando will get $250,000 and ten percent of the gross. Paramount flirts with the idea of distributing the picture, but the studio is nervous, rightly foreseeing an X rating. So independent distributor United Artists agrees to handle it.

The picture is shot in Paris in the winter of 1971–72. The role of the girl, Jeanne, has gone to Maria Schneider, the nineteen-year-old daughter of Daniel Gélin, one of Brando's old Parisian friends. They meet and engage in a staring contest—how could they not when the actors know what is expected of them? If anything has got Schneider the role it is the uninhibited way she tosses off her clothes during an audition. The nakedness will not be an issue for her. She calls Brando "Daddy," and in time there will be an affair between them. How could there not be on such a film, with such frankness, when Schneider is the very type of girl Brando might fall for—dark, voluptuous, insolent yet ultimately dependent?

Let it be said, there is a ferment in filmmaking at this time on the overlap between fiction and documentary, and the challenge to audiences to discern one from the other. At the heart of this debate, of course, is the whole question of whether acting is a matter of skilled pretense or a mining into real personality. Everything about the artistic approach to *Last Tango in Paris*, from the hiring of Brando to the way the script is colored by his long talks with Bertolucci, promises an unrivaled (if ambiguous) portrait of the actor as human being.

Just before shooting begins, Bertolucci sees a major exhibit of paintings by Francis Bacon. This has an influence on his vision of the film. He tries to adapt Bacon's idea of large lonely figures, monstrous in their passion, like raw meat on the edge of being tortured souls. The burnt browns and blood reds of Bacon's palette also contribute to the look of the film, as photographed by Vittorio Storaro and designed by Ferdinando Scarfiotti. Thus, the film has a highly fabricated look that is already somewhat at odds with the intended spontaneity of the action. Indeed, as *The Conformist* shows, Bertolucci is a very style-conscious director—by no means a documentarian.

Already, some people close to Brando have warned him that in language and action this script is dangerously close to being "pornographic." No one

The Odd Trio
The parties in one of the screen's great sexual explorations—director Bernardo Bertolucci and stars Brando and Maria Schneider discuss a moment from *Last Tango in Paris*.

Just Pretending
"I never felt any sexual attraction to Brando," Maria Schneider (in a scene from *Last Tango*) later said. "He was very uptight about his weight."

ever knows or says what the word means—beyond the warning that such a film would not get an acceptable rating, and is "beneath" a professional actor of Brando's quality. But a day comes, and very likely Bertolucci has known this, when the director says that he wants Brando and Schneider to be Paul and Jeanne to this drastic extent—they are to have real sex. Brando objects, and claims to be hurt, saying that such a thing would make the sexual organs characters in the film.

Well, perhaps, but what is a film about the roots of sex to do? The request from Bertolucci is not unreasonable. After all, Schneider is stark naked for much of the film; she will be seen being sodomized, or in simulated sodomy. Whereas Brando keeps his clothes on. There is some value in this contrast: for it makes the girl seem younger, purer, more innocent, while the man is so scarred by life he needs clothes. But there is a possibility lost or evaded by this: it is of Brando and Schneider equally naked, equally exposed and committed.

Of course, *Last Tango* is not quite that. Schneider will later complain that she was exploited, and she has a point. Brando is never naked, no matter that adoring critics will praise his emotional exposure. Apparently, there were shots of his private parts filmed, but Bertolucci cuts them from his own film, as if shy of violating the icon or the paternal figure's status. So *Last Tango* becomes no more than a riveting film about an affair in which the advantages given the man in the film's bias add to our sense of the necessity in which this helpless young woman must murder him.

Opening at the New York Film Festival in the fall of 1972, and going public the following year, *Last Tango* is already a scandal. In Italy itself, suits are filed against the filmmakers for "obscenity." There are fierce debates over censoring it. Pauline Kael is one writer who defends the film with all her might. She calls it "the most powerfully erotic film ever made," and she sees it as personal redemption for Brando. As never before since *A Streetcar Named Desire*, Brando has reclaimed his poetic persona—that of someone stranded between brutishness and the Dionysian impulse. It surely assists this that his face has not seemed so lean or pensive in years. This is the last time when people will, unhesitatingly, call him "beautiful."

The film earns $45 million, ensuring Brando of at least an extra $4 million. And despite its scandalous nature, it wins Oscar nominations for Director and Actor. (Bertolucci loses to George Roy Hill for *The Sting*, and Brando to Jack Lemmon for *Save the Tiger*.)

Like most scandals, the film has dated. Its sex is very much of 1972. There is regular intercourse and the sodomy, but there is no oral sex and there is no kind of role-playing. It does not really say very much that is profound and general about sex—how could it, really, for sex belongs to us all. But as a tragic melodrama about a desperate affair it is remarkable and very moving.

And as a half-masked portrait of Marlon Brando is it essential. For here, close to fifty, the man already half-buried in his own debris, faces the harsh limitation to his kind of acting. The deliberate confusion of Brando's life with that of his character leads to a blurring. The part begs to be better written. His desperation needs to go further. The Method—its reality, its truth, its fusion of life and art, those things need to be set aside. Acting is pretending. *Last Tango* could be as fearsome as *King Lear*—yet it ends up as only a gesture towards that pain. But Brando has had his chance, he has gone to the shore of El Dorado (the infinitely remote island that is treasure itself) and he has been forced to return to the old life. He has been too cautious, too prim, too much Vito Corleone when in sight of the beast itself.

Forbidden Hit

Controversy sells magazines as well as films—so it was no surprise when *Time* put Brando on its cover with a story about the racy scenes in *Last Tango*.

Long Twilight
1974–2002

MISSOURI BREAKDOWN

It's natural, after *The Godfather* and *Last Tango*, that supporters should assume renewal in a man still not fifty years old. For here are two performances at opposite extremes, the one set in the classic mold of Hollywood acting, the other perhaps the most radical, dangerous thing a great star has ever done. It takes a little time, therefore, before the world appreciates that *Last Tango* is an ending. At which point, its opening cry of horror, "Fucking God!" on the Bir-Hakeim bridge in Paris, signals retreat as much as the character's frenzied effort to bring on his own death.

There is a gap of four years before he works again, which already indicates despair. He spends more time in Tahiti and helping the cause of the Indian; he tries to repair his family; he has many other affairs. And he makes gestures at acting again. When a sequel to *The Godfather* is proposed, he demands so much money as to eliminate himself. Why not? He feels he was cheated on the first film—he may even admit that he was his own betrayer.

So he does not act again until *The Missouri Breaks* (1976). It is a Western, written by the novelist Thomas McGuane, directed by Arthur Penn, and produced by Elliott Kastner. As his co-star, Brando is to have Jack Nicholson, one of his best admirers and a neighbor up on Mulholland Drive. Brando stipulates that he will consider only a very limited shoot (five weeks, with penalties for any delays). He is to receive $1.25 million and a percentage, and he turns up on the appointed day—the film is under way

HIS NEIGHBOR JACK

Of all the actors who grew up in the tradition of Marlon Brando, none has been more dedicated than Jack Nicholson. Their naturalistic styles are alike; they are both known as men with an appreciative eye for the ladies; and they are neighbors on Mulholland Drive (the properties have a shared entrance). But Nicholson admitted to feeling overawed as they came to work together on *The Missouri Breaks*. Then, as Brando came to their scenes together, asking for cue cards, but then

Besides homes in Los Angeles, Nicholson and Brando (acting in *The Missouri Breaks*) own adjoining condos on the Pacific island of Bora Bora.

inventing new dialogue as they filmed, Nicholson was taken aback. It was a friendly battle, the two men stayed in character, but onlookers had to believe they were seeing a kind of sparring between two championship actors. In the story, Jack cuts Marlon's throat, but in the mood of it all, Marlon came away undefeated.

already—at the Billings, Montana, location driving his own extensively appointed Winnebago, larger than anyone has foreseen. This is a little like his character, the regulator, Robert Lee Clayton, hired to expunge the Breaks country of rustlers and rogues—notably the gang led by Nicholson.

The script is incomplete and Brando immediately tells Arthur Penn that he doesn't really see who his character is. So they agree to make that problem an asset: let Lee Clayton be mercurial, slippery to a degree, a man of disguises, accents—an actor's lovely exercise. And so Brando seeks buckskins and a sombrero; he makes Lee Clayton the swishest killer who ever rode the West; he has an exquisite Irish accent, but it is always likely to turn southern or . . . like nothing on Earth. He has a relationship with his horse. He plays the flute. He is a bird-spotter. He wears a bonnet and a dress when it suits him. He is nothing less than an audacious, insolent master-actor turned loose on a defunct American genre.

It will be said that Brando "ruins" *The Missouri Breaks* because he reduces its natural untidiness to the condition of a woolen garment unraveling before your eyes. Certainly the picture is a big failure. On the other hand, this is a Western in which a character refers to the eighteenth-century novel *Tristram Shandy*; it is a drama of power and revenge (if you will) always on the point of turning into an absurdist comedy. And who is guiding it that way—as if he were offering a sweet apple to a dumb nag? Why, Marlon Brando. Here is Brando's most outright comic performance. Here is proof that the hulk can do anything. A lighter touch on the film, a more coherently comic script, and *The Missouri Breaks* could have been superb. For now, it is simply a marvel. I say "for now" because it is a movie that gets steadily better and it is a rare example of how chaos during shooting may lead to something rare.

But as it is, Brando gets a lot of the blame—in part this is understandable. Brando's insouciance, his discarding of "script" in favor of whim, has not made the shooting easier or more economical. He has walked off the set sometimes when he is not amused. The delays have mounted. He has been infuriating. And his deal, on the gross, means that he walks away from the wrecked film with about $16.5 million. This is not wholesome or good for the film business, yet Brando has already decided that the film business is a rotting corpse beyond rescue. His explanation to himself is that the wretchedly won money may help his island and his Indians. And perhaps it does. At the same time, he begins to spread contempt and malice in the very art he may be better equipped to save.

Superman (1978) is uglier still, by far. Playing father to Christopher Reeve, Brando is engaged for two pictures—they are to be shot simultaneously.

Superdad

Brando told director Richard Donner that he wanted to play Superman's father (opposite Susannah York) as "a green suitcase." In fact, he took the part seriously—and got his lines right on the first take.

FRANCIS FORD COPPOLA
PRESENTS

Apocalypse Now

MARLON BRANDO ROBERT DUVALL MARTIN SHEEN in APOCALYPSE NOW
FREDERIC FORREST ALBERT HALL SAM BOTTOMS LARRY FISHBURNE and DENNIS HOPPER
Produced and Directed by FRANCIS COPPOLA
Written by JOHN MILIUS and FRANCIS COPPOLA Narration by MICHAEL HERR
Co-Produced by FRED ROOS, GRAY FREDERICKSON and TOM STERNBERG
Director of Photography VITTORIO STORARO Production Designer DEAN TAVOULARIS Editor RICHARD MARKS
Sound Design by WALTER MURCH Music by CARMINE COPPOLA and FRANCIS COPPOLA
R RESTRICTED TECHNICOLOR® DD DOLBY STEREO United Artists AN OMNI ZOETROPE PRODUCTION

Up the River

Apocalypse Now had so many production delays that wags in Hollywood dubbed the unseen film *Apocalypse, When?* The ad campaign, including this poster, played up Brando's involvement.

He will be paid $3.7 million for this, plus 11.3 percent of the U.S. gross and 5.6 percent of the foreign gross. He wears a robe that avoids all questions about his size. He works twelve days and is on screen for fifteen minutes. The producers include no footage of Brando in *Superman II* (1980). And it is reckoned that he goes away finally with $15 million for his cameo.

By now, that is all there is to be said about *Superman*: the numbers are more momentous and more interesting than the performance, which is as routine as the picture is foolish. *Superman* makes a fortune and the world of movies is turning away from seriousness with the discovery of a young audience asking for no more. So Brando can persuade himself that he is justified in all he does. But that is only possible because he is so detached from his own nature and the way a few people regard him.

UP THE RIVER

In 1979's *Apocalypse Now*, Colonel Walter R. Kurtz is said to have been "one of the most outstanding officers this country's ever produced . . . And he was a good man, too." I doubt this metaphor was ever intended, by those who wrote the script or made the film, but it seems uncanny now how far the description fits Brando. The general who primes Captain Willard (Martin Sheen) to find and eliminate Kurtz, reasons thus: "Sometimes the dark side overcomes what Lincoln called the better angels of our nature."

Kurtz has cracked. Sent into the field in Vietnam, he has taken his band of Montagnard tribesmen into Cambodia, where he has his own unruly kingdom. Now, Willard's order is to terminate this outlaw "with extreme prejudice." The story comes from Joseph Conrad's *Heart of Darkness*, but the situation is brilliantly transposed to illumine the war in Vietnam and the way American duty (or arrogance) has taken a country to the edge of hell.

It begins as a reunion of friends: Brando agrees to play Kurtz—four weeks' work—for $3.5 million (after all, Kurtz appears only at the end of the picture and most of his scenes can be done on a single set). Coppola has told himself in advance that *Apocalypse Now* should be a holiday and a picnic.

Then everything goes wrong. Harvey Keitel has to be replaced by Martin Sheen. There is a typhoon that destroys sets. They are in the Philippines where everything is slow and difficult and expensive. And Francis Coppola is financing this film himself (to ensure that he ends up making more from it). But that means that as the budget mounts (from $5 million to over $25 million), the director has to carry the loans and the strain. He suffers enormously and has a kind of breakdown.

Thus, before Brando's arrival (the final session), Coppola calls the actor, the old friend, and negotiates. Brando could not be more accommodating: yes, he will now do five weeks and take only $1 million up front— plus 11.3 percent of the gross profits. The original contract had two other stipulations: that Brando will come to work far less heavy than he has been lately; and that he will have read the Conrad novella to prepare himself for Kurtz.

Pause a moment: Francis Coppola was not always behaving well or rationally on *Apocalypse Now*. He is a manipulative artist—he is a film director. It is quite possible that Brando had seen and felt an unworthy side of Coppola. On the other hand, the director had rescued the actor with *The Godfather*. They had stood firm together against constant threats to protect the film. And the film had been good. Brando had taken an inferior deal on the picture—but that was all his doing.

He comes to the Philippines enormous: the minimum guess is 250 pounds. He has not looked at the book. It is true that Coppola's script for the Kurtz scenes is neither clear nor coherent. But the line of the film is plain, and just as plain is Coppola's desperate condition. He needs a great actor's rescue and assistance. Instead, Brando launches into immense, stagnant debates on the script, the theme and Kurtz's madness. The delays are made greater. The filming turns nightmarish. A scheme is worked out where Brando is seen as just highlights in darkness. In the end, there is an extraordinary quality in the Kurtz scenes, but not a great deal of clarity. Instead, one is beholding the ruminations of a windy actor. It is not pretty, and it is not professional or gracious.

Inadvertently, though, a portrait emerges of a great inflated genius who has gone up the river or away to an island and is consumed in his flatulent rhetoric. As so often, one sees glimpses of what Brando has

ELEANOR'S NOTES

Eleanor Coppola reported that during the intense filming of *Apocalypse Now*, Brando threw a party at the resort where he was staying; four hundred people came.

In *Notes*, her book about the making of *Apocalypse Now*, Francis Coppola's wife Eleanor wrote of the shock felt by everyone on the crew to find Brando so overweight, and so unprepared. But Eleanor also admitted the actor's astonishing power and presence: "He seemed to be looking at me in microscopic detail . . . Not in a judgmental way. Just in complete absorption of all the details . . . Being in Marlon's presence is not neutral. What a burden it must be for him to have hardly anyone who feels completely natural around him."

In His Own Words

Brando did not much conceal the fact that his autobiography was taken on as a way to meet the costs of son Christian's trial. Nor did he hide his own initial reluctance to write the book. He entertained the notion (surely fascinating) that he would enlist fifteen or twenty of the most notable women in his life to write a chapter each. But the publisher, Random House, with $4 million at stake as an advance, could

Brando (with Christian and Miko in 1990) used the proceeds from his autobiography to pay for Christian's legal defense.

not risk the book being so diffuse. Brando had difficulty with the writing and after two years he approached Robert Lindsey to help him. (Lindsey had previously helped Ronald Reagan in a similar task.) Lindsey talked to Brando for weeks, about any topic—except that Brando did not like to name his girlfriends.

brought to a role. But now the revelations are embarrassing. One begins to feel the authentic horror of what Marlon Brando has become.

For anyone in doubt, wait a few years for his own book and this revolting account of that encounter: "I was good at bullshitting Francis and persuading him to think my way, and he bought it, but what I'd really wanted from the beginning was to find a way to make my part smaller so that I wouldn't have to work as hard."

All or Nothing

Do not expect an actor to be the master of his revels. If Marlon Brando has reached the conclusion that it is impossible to do honest or honorable work, do not let his own many shortcomings rule out that conclusion. He may be right. He may claim, with justice, that much of his life has been striving to demonstrate the inadequacy—the crimes even—of Hollywood.

In the years since *Apocalypse Now*, it has been his habit to work occasionally, for as short a schedule as possible and for as much money. Or for virtually nothing   as if to make a parable of himself.

After watching Alex Haley's *Roots* on television in 1977, he agrees to play George Lincoln Rockwell in the 1979-80 sequel, *Roots: The Next Generation*—one day's work for $25,000, and that given straight to charity. He wins an Emmy, and it is a thoughtful if finally opaque performance.

But then there is *The Formula* (1980), in which he plays a clichéd villain in a melodrama opposite George C. Scott (one of the few actors of his time in his class)—ten days work for $3 million.

Then, after nine years away comes *A Dry White Season* (1989), playing a South African lawyer pledged to resist apartheid. He does it for scale and donates that small sum to charity.

The only one of the last films with charm or quality is *The Freshman* (1990). He gets $3.3 million and 11 percent of the gross—but by now, of course $3 million is not so much. And for once, he really acts a whole part, a benevolent Mafia father figure, a fond parody of Vito Corleone, and a nice opportunity for dainty amusement. He is worth the fee.

Christopher Columbus: The Discovery (1992) is ignominious—$5 million for ten minutes on screen in a film that sustains every old Western notion about the

Just Kidding

While shooting *The Freshman* in Toronto, Brando blasted the film in an interview, calling it "a stinker." Costar Matthew Broderick was furious; when the film started to look like a hit, Brando retracted his comments.

NOT COMING TO A THEATER NEAR YOU

Brave **director Johnny Depp** (in Cannes with the film's composer, Iggy Pop) got to know Brando while making *Don Juan de Marco*.

*T*he *Brave* was a real movie, shown at the Cannes Film Festival in 1997, but seldom elsewhere. Brando's role in it is not large, but the plot of the picture clearly shows his influence. Johnny Depp plays an American Indian, Raphael, drunk and so poor that he agrees to be murdered for money. As such, the movie offers a grimly realistic portrait of Indian life—itself no great

encouragement to a young audience set on escapism. Depp also directed the film, and all reports are that it is beautiful but very slow and obscure; it was never properly distributed. Brando plays a man in a wheelchair who ruminates with Raphael on the nature of death.

place of Indian culture. He is rebuked by many of the Indians he has defended, but he says he has no choice. *Columbus* coincides with the plight of his own family.

And others: *Don Juan de Marco* (1995), passable; *The Island of Dr. Moreau* (1996), grotesque; *The Brave* (1997) and *Free Money* (1997), scarcely released; and *The Score* (2001), with Robert De Niro and Edward Norton, a film in which Brando has to sigh after every three words and scarcely seems able to move. He seems closer to 350 pounds. And he seems to have passed beyond his own control or attention. Does he even know he is there?

DEAD CALM

There is no natural justice, and thus no way of saying that anyone deserves what happens, or has earned it. But in actorly people there is sometimes a theatrical energy that can lead to melodrama in real life. Actors think

Island Guy

In *The Island of Dr. Moreau*, Brando may have hit a career low, while tipping the scales to new heights.

in story arcs, and sometimes those curves appear in their sky, like rainbows or warnings.

On May 16, 1990, Christian Brando is thirty-two and terribly unresolved. That evening, in his father's house on Mulholland Drive, Christian shoots and kills Dag Drollet, the lover of his half-sister, Cheyenne. Marlon is in the house, along with Tarita, his third wife, and his housekeeper, Cristina Ruiz, by whom Brando has already had the first of two baby girls. Drollet is the son of Jacques Drollet, the man who had once opposed Marlon's purchase of the island of Teti'aroa.

Brando calls the police, and then he calls the lawyer William Kunstler. Cheyenne is several months pregnant with Dag's child—that child is born in June 1990 and is immediately diagnosed as a drug addict. Later, the child will be given to the custody of Tarita because of the instability of Cheyenne.

Brando uses his house to guarantee bail for Christian, and not long thereafter he undertakes to write his autobiography for Random House for $4 million.

Christian is convicted after a trial in which Marlon is an often tearful witness. People wonder whether he was acting or was himself on the stand. Christian is sentenced to ten years.

Four years later, very overweight, Cheyenne hangs herself on the Brando estate in Tahiti.

Marlon Brando lives still on Mulholland Drive and on the island of Teti'aroa. In April 2003, he will be seventy-nine. There is no need for films or plays. The natural tragedy affects us all, whether it arouses anger, pity or helplessness. The most dynamic actor of our age has been stilled, and surely the terrible burden of acting has added to this dead calm.

In the fall of 2001, operating out of his own house, he proposes to offer a class on acting. In dark robes and a flowing pink scarf, he sits in a thronelike armchair and utters remarks on his art. There is an extraordinary mixture of the profound and the portentous. But what does anyone expect at this stage of his life? He is not doing the class for its own sake. He is hard up again, and he has eyes on a DVD from the sessions, a tool to be sold. Moreover, he calls the sessions "Lying for a Living," as if something very deep down forbade him from taking his own great talent seriously. He seems to be warning his students about

THE MANSO BOOK

Brando (in a photo circa 1952) has had literary aspirations since his early career; he often claimed to have written (or started to write) several books.

Peter Manso's *Brando: The Biography* was published in 1994, at 1,118 pages. It was done without Brando's help, of course, but it is unlikely to be rivaled as the most comprehensive account of the life. The research is extraordinary, and the tone is actually very sympathetic. But when Brando read the book (or parts of it), he is said to have cried out "This guy wants to be me! Why would anyone want to be me!" A chance remark, perhaps, but so deeply discerning of how a couple of generations have regarded Marlon Brando, and of the terrible difficulty he has living with himself.

the racket and the con they seek to enter—yet, at the same time, he is saying "Don't trust me."

Many notable actors attend the classes. But Brando is not the sole director of events. The British film director Tony Kaye (the maker of the troubled *American History X)* is actually handling the camera at the classes. He attends dressed as Osama bin Laden (just weeks after September 11). That offends some people, yet Kaye asks, "Aren't we concerned with acting?"

But then Kaye breaks away from Brando and is said to mount his own mock-classes, with a 500-pound man impersonating Brando. The split ends in fierce legal troubles as Brando has to sue in an attempt to recover the footage from his own venture. Does it mean that most of us will never see the coverage of a great actor in the eccentric role of teacher, never be in the position of trying to distinguish the gold from the dross?

In which case, does this calamity sound accidental—or is it something the terrible, wounded cynic in Brando has contrived? Is his woeful size simply the consequence of his loss of self-respect and control, or is it a violence against our memory of his beauty?

All of this is part of the absorbing, ongoing glory and tragedy in being Marlon Brando. It may be, in the long run, that his signal achievement is not just in his roles—great and stupid—but in the way he has allowed us to step back from actor-worship to ask the tricky questions: What is an actor? And why should we have come to prefer them to real people? He may be the genius and the barbarian who first helped expose the cult of acting.

The Next Generation
Brando and Sean Penn in 1998. For several years, Penn's company was trying to make a movie of *The Autumn of the Patriarch* by Gabriel Garcia Marquez with Brando in the lead.

Filmography

Includes director, principal cast besides Brando, and Academy Award wins or nominations for Brando

1950   **The Men** (dir. Fred Zinnemann)
Teresa Wright, Everett Sloane, Jack Webb,
Richard Erdman, Arthur Jurado, Virginia Farmer

1951   **A Streetcar Named Desire** (pictured at right;
dir. Elia Kazan; Oscar nomination for actor)
Vivien Leigh, Karl Malden, Kim Hunter

1952   **Viva Zapata!** (dir. Elia Kazan; Oscar
nomination for actor)
Jean Peters, Anthony Quinn, Joseph Wiseman,
Arnold Moss, Alan Reed, Margo, Frank Silvera

1953   **Julius Caesar** (dir. Joseph L. Mankiewicz;
Oscar nomination for actor)
James Mason, John Gielgud, Louis Calhern, Edmond
O'Brien, Greer Garson, Deborah Kerr, George Macready

1954   **The Wild One** (dir. László Benedek)
Mary Murphy, Lee Marvin, Robert Keith, Jay C. Flippen

On the Waterfront (dir. Elia Kazan; Oscar win
for actor)
Eva Marie Saint, Karl Malden, Lee J. Cobb, Rod
Steiger, Pat Henning, Leif Erickson

Desirée (dir. Henry Koster)
Jean Simmons, Merle Oberon, Michael Rennie,
Cameron Mitchell, Elizabeth Sellars

1955   **Guys and Dolls** (dir. Joseph L. Mankiewicz)
Jean Simmons, Frank Sinatra, Vivian Blaine, Robert
Keith, Stubby Kaye, Regis Toomey, Veda Ann Borg,
Sheldon Leonard

1956   **The Teahouse of the August Moon**
(dir. Daniel Mann)
Glenn Ford, Machiko Kyo, Eddie Albert, Paul Ford,
Jun Negami, Henry Morgan

1957   **Sayonara** (dir. Joshua Logan; Oscar nomination
for actor)
Patricia Owens, James Garner, Martha Scott, Miiko

Taka, Miyoshi Umeki, Red Buttons, Kent Smith,
Ricardo Montalban

1958   **The Young Lions** (dir. Edward Dmytryk)
Montgomery Clift, Dean Martin, Hope Lange,
Barbara Rush, May Britt, Maximilian Schell, Dora
Doll, Lee Van Cleef, Liliane Montevecchi

1960   **The Fugitive Kind** (dir. Sidney Lumet)
Joanne Woodward, Anna Magnani, Maureen
Stapleton, Victor Jory, R.G. Armstrong

1961   **One-Eyed Jacks** (also directed)
Karl Malden, Katy Jurado, Pina Pellicer, Ben
Johnson, Slim Pickens, Timothy Carey, Miriam
Colon, Elisha Cook Jr.

1962   **Mutiny on the Bounty** (dir. Lewis Milestone)
Trevor Howard, Richard Harris, Tarita, Hugh
Griffith, Richard Haydn, Gordon Jackson

1963   **The Ugly American** (dir. George Englund)
Eiji Okada, Sandra Church, Pat Hingle, Arthur Hill,
Jocelyn Brando, Judson Pratt, Reiko Sato

1964   **Bedtime Story** (dir. Ralph Levy)
David Niven, Shirley Jones, Dody Goodman, Marie
Windsor

1965   **Morituri** (dir. Bernhard Wicki)
Yul Brynner, Janet Margolin, Trevor Howard,
Martin Benrath, Hans Christian, Wally Cox

1966   **The Chase** (dir. Arthur Penn)
Jane Fonda, Robert Redford, E.G. Marshall, Angie
Dickinson, Janice Rule, Miriam Hopkins, Martha Hyer,
Richard Bradford, Robert Duvall, James Fox,
Jocelyn Brando

The Appaloosa (dir. Sidney J. Furie)
Anjanette Comer, John Saxon, Emilio Fernandez,
Alex Montoya, Miriam Colon, Rafael Campos,
Frank Silvera

1967 **The Countess from Hong Kong**
(dir. Charles Chaplin)
Sophia Loren, Sydney Chaplin, Tippi Hedren, Patrick Cargill, Michael Medwin, Margaret Rutherford

Reflections in a Golden Eye (dir. John Huston)
Elizabeth Taylor, Brian Keith, Julie Harris, Robert Forster, Zorro David

1968 **Candy** (dir. Christian Marquand)
Ewa Aulin, Charles Aznavour, Richard Burton, James Coburn, John Huston, Walter Matthau, Ringo Starr, John Astin, Elsa Martinelli, Sugar Ray Robinson, Anita Pallenberg

1969 **The Night of the Following Day**
(dir. Hubert Cornfield)
Richard Boone, Rita Moreno, Pamela Franklin

Burn! (dir. Gillo Pontecorvo)
Evaristo Marquez, Norman Hill, Renato Salvatori

1971 **The Nightcomers** (dir. Michael Winner)
Harry Andrews, Stephanie Beacham, Christopher Ellis, Thora Hird

1972 **The Godfather** (dir. Francis Ford Coppola; Oscar win for actor)
Al Pacino, Diane Keaton, Robert Duvall, James Caan, Sterling Hayden, Talia Shire, Richard Conte, Abe Vigoda, John Cazale, Al Martino

1973 **Last Tango in Paris** (dir. Bernardo Bertolucci; Oscar nomination for actor)
Maria Schneider, Maria Michi, Giovanni Galletti, Gitt Magrini, Catherine Allegret, Luce Marquand, Marie-Helene Breillat, Catherine Breillat, Jean-Pierre Leaud

1976 **The Missouri Breaks** (pictured at left; dir. Arthur Penn)
Jack Nicholson, Randy Quaid, Kathleen Lloyd, Frederic Forrest, Harry Dean Stanton, John McLiam, John P. Ryan

1978 **Superman** (dir. Richard Donner)
Christopher Reeve, Gene Hackman, Ned Beatty, Jackie Cooper, Glenn Ford, Trevor Howard, Margot Kidder, Valerie Perrine, Maria Schell, Terence Stamp, Susannah York

1979 **Raoni** (dir. Jean-Pierre Dutilleux, Luiz Carlos Saldanha; English language narrator only)

Apocalypse Now (dir. Francis Ford Coppola)
Martin Sheen, Robert Duvall, Frederic Forrest, Sam Bottoms, Laurence Fishburne, Dennis Hopper, G.D. Spradlin, Harrison Ford, Scott Glenn, Albert Hall

1980 **The Formula** (dir. John G. Avildsen)
George C. Scott, Marthe Keller, John Gielgud, Beatrice Straight

1989 **A Dry White Season** (dir. Euzhan Palcy; Oscar nomination for supporting actor)
Donald Sutherland, Susan Sarandon, Janet Suzman, Zakes Mokae, Jurgen Prochnow, Winston Ntshona

1990 **The Freshman** (dir. Andrew Bergman)
Matthew Broderick, Bruno Kirby, Penelope Ann Miller, Frank Whaley, Jon Polito, B.D. Wong, Maximilian Schell, Paul Benedict, Kenneth Welsh, Pamela Payton-Wright

1992 **Christopher Columbus: The Discovery**
(dir. John Glen)
Tom Selleck, George Corraface, Rachel Ward, Robert Davi, Catherine Zeta-Jones, Oliver Cotton, Benicio Del Toro

1995 **Don Juan DeMarco** (dir. Jeremy Leven)
Johnny Depp, Faye Dunaway, Geraldine Pailhas, Bob Dishy, Rachel Ticotin, Talisa Soto

1996 **The Island of Dr. Moreau**
(dir. John Frankenheimer, Ralph Stanley)
Val Kilmer, David Thewlis, Fairuza Balk, Ron Perlman

1997 **The Brave** (dir. Johnny Depp)
Johnny Depp, Marshall Bell, Elpidia Carrillo, Frederic Forrest, Clarence Williams III, Max Perlich, Luis Guzman

1998 **Free Money** (dir. Yves Simoneau)
Charles Sheen, Thomas Haden, Donald Sutherland, Martin Sheen, David Arquette

2001 **The Score** (dir. Frank Oz, Robert DeNiro)
Robert De Niro, Edward Norton, Angela Bassett

Photo Credits

Page #/ Position	Credit	Page #/ Position	Credit	Page #/ Position	Credit
1	Trapper Frank/ Corbis Sygma	46	Gordon Anthony/ Getty Images	114-119	Photofest
2-3	Photofest	47	Alfred Eisenstaedt/ Pix Inc./TimePix	120	AP Photo
4-5	Lawrence Thornton/ Getty Images	48	Leonard McCombe/TimePix	121-135	Photofest
6	Photofest			136	Bettmann/Corbis
7	Hulton Archive/ Getty Images	49	Hulton Archive/ Getty Images	137	Time Magazine, Copyright Time Inc./TimePix
8-9	Library of Congress	50-51	Hulton Archive/ Getty Images	138-139	DMI/TimePix
10	Lisa Larsen/TimePix			140-143	Photofest
11	Hulton Archive/ Getty Images	52	Photofest	144	Kevin Winter/DMI/TimePix
		53	Bettmann/Corbis		
12	Photofest	54-55	Hulton Archive/ Getty Images	145-146	Photofest
13	Hulton Archive/ Getty Images			147	Cardinale Stephane/ Corbis Sygma
		56-57	Photofest		
14	Photofest	58	John Springer Collection/Corbis	148	Photofest
15	AP Photo			149	AP Photo
16	Hulton Archive/ Getty Images	59-60	Photofest	150-151	Photofest
		61	Bettmann/Corbis	152-153	Photofest
17	Art Shay/TimePix	62-64	Photofest		
18-19	Lawrence Thornton/ Getty Images	65	Hulton Archive/ Getty Images		
20-21	Photofest	66-69	Photofest		
22	AP Photo	70	Elder Neville/ Corbis Sygma		
22-28	Photofest	71-82	Photofest		
29	Bettmann/Corbis	83	Hulton Archive/TimePix		
30	Photofest	84-85	AP Photo		
31	Yves Forestier/ Corbis Sygma	85-91	Photofest		
32	Hulton Archive/ Getty Images	92-93	Gene Lester/Getty Images		
		94-96	Photofest		
33	Tony Linck/TimePix	96-97	Hulton Archive/ Getty Images		
34	Eileen Darby/TimePix				
35	Photofest	98-102	Photofest		
36	Hulton Archive/ Getty Images	103	Grey Villett/TimePix		
		104-105	Photofest		
37-39	Photofest	106-107	Photofest		
40-41	Bettmann/Corbis	108	Hulton Archive/ Getty Images		
42-43	Photofest				
44-45	Frank Schershell/TimePix	109-112	Photofest		
45	Photofest	113	Bettmann/Corbis		

Acknowledgements

The publishers would like to thank A&E Networks, Avalon Publishing Group, and their associates for their hard work and good humor throughout this project. Special thanks go to Max Alexander, Tracy Armstead, and Lisa Vaughn for efforts above and beyond the call of duty, and to Sean Moore, f-stop fitzgerald, and Will Balliett for their vision in conceiving this series and their determination to make it a reality. We would also like to extend our continued appreciation to ColourScan Ltd., Singapore, for their excellent work.

Avalon Publishing Group would like to thank Judith McQuown, Jonathan Gregg, and Nanette Cardon for their efforts on this project, as well as the kind cooperation of Hilary Johnston at TimePix, Yvette Reyes at AP Wide World Photo, Colombe Meurin at Photos12.com, and Valerie Zars at Hulton Getty. At DK, Chuck Lang for his support; Chuck Wills for his dogged pursuit of accuracy and good writing; Dirk Kaufman for his great design eye and Gregor Hall for keeping things moving with patience and understanding. At AETN, Juan Davila, Chey Blake, Charles Wright, Liz Durkin and David Walmsley all helped put the pieces together, Cindy Berenson kept the ball rolling with her grateful professionalism and, most of all, thanks to Carrie Trimmer, who has supported this series and has contributed to it in so many ways above and beyond the call.

Additional Captions

pg. 1:   The Academy Awards Oscar trophy, which Marlon Brando has been awarded twice.

pg. 2-3   Marlon Brando and Jean Simmons in a publicity shot for the 1955 film production of *Guys and Dolls.*

pg. 4-5:   A dramatic nighttime view of New York City's Theater District in the 1940s, when the young Marlon Brando blasts onto the American scene.

pg. 8-9:   Omaha, Nebraska (seen in 1916) has long been an important transportation center on the Missouri River. The state is famous for raising corn, football players, and unexpected actors.

pg. 18-19:   By 1945, when this photo was taken, Manhattan had replaced New Orleans as the jazz capital of the world. Its nightclubs and recording studios were meccas of musical innovation.

pg. 40-41:   Marlon Brando as Stanley Kowalski and Vivien Leigh as Blanche DuBois in the 1951 film version of *A Streetcar Named Desire.*

pg. 54-55:   The famous Hollywood sign is only a few miles down the road from Brando's hilltop home above Los Angeles.

pg. 92-93:   Paramount Pictures and the famous Bronson Gate, in Hollywood. When Brando made *One-Eyed Jacks* there, the studio was run by its scrappy founder, Adolph Zukor. By the time of *The Godfather,* it was a division of Gulf + Western.

pg. 106-107: Always one to upstage his costars, Brando was occasionally bested, as in this scene from the 1964 film *Bedtime Story.* Is it any wonder he disdained his profession?

pg. 126-127: Brando, as Vito Corleone, gets a grip on singer Johnny Fontane (played by singer Al Martino) during the first reel of *The Godfather.* It was Brando's idea to slap Martino.

pg. 138-139: Brando greets a photographer on the set of the 1990 film *The Freshman.* He got along better with his young costar, Matthew Broderick.

Index